THE TURQUOISE ELEPHANT
STEPHEN CARLETON

CURRENCY PRESS
SYDNEY

GRIFFIN
THEATRE
COMPANY

CURRENT THEATRE SERIES

First published in 2016
by Currency Press Pty Ltd,
PO Box 2287, Strawberry Hills, NSW, 2012, Australia
enquiries@currency.com.au
www.currency.com.au

in association with Griffin Theatre Company

Cataloguing-in-publication data for this title is available from the National
Library of Australia website: www.nla.gov.au

Typeset by Dean Nottle for Currency Press.
Front cover shows Catherine Davies.
Cover photograph by Brett Boardman.
Cover design by RE:.

Currency Press acknowledges the Traditional Owners of the Country on which
we live and work. We pay our respects to all Aboriginal and Torres Strait
Islander Elders, past and present.

Contents

ACKNOWLEDGEMENTS

The Turquoise Elephant was developed with the support of Playwriting Australia and the University of Sydney's Department of Performance Studies. I would like to thank Laura Ginters and Tim Roseman for brokering this wonderful dramaturgical development opportunity, and for providing such excellent insight and theatrical intelligence themselves in the room. Thanks to all of the actors, interns and students who participated in that process and moved the piece in positive directions during that critical stage of its development.

Thank you also to Ben Winspear and Melanie Carolan for being part of that dramaturgical process at the University of Sydney and throughout, and to Lee Lewis and the whole team at Griffin (Karen, Will, Elliott, Aurora, Lane—everyone!) who supported the play during its development and production, and for responding so wonderfully to the text in the first instance. Being selected for production always feels like something of a miracle. I appreciate the opportunity deeply.

Thank you finally to Gale Edwards. Your razor sharp and unflagging perception and theatrical savvy—your unrelenting eye for the story have made this play so much better than it would have been without you. Thank you for bringing the superb Brian Thomson to the design table with you. Two theatre legends for the price of—well, half a one probably! I'm blessed. Thanks, Lee, for introducing us.

Stephen Carleton

*For Hugo, as always. And hoping your
future's a bit brighter than this one.*

The Turquoise Elephant was first produced by Griffin Theatre Company at SBW Stables Theatre, Sydney, on 14 October 2016, with the following cast:

VISI	Catherine Davies
AUGUSTA	Maggie Dence
JEFF	Julian Garner
OLYMPIA	Belinda Giblin
BASRA	Olivia Rose
MASKED FIGURE	iOTA

Director, Gale Edwards
Set Designer, Brian Thomson
Costume Designer, Emma Vine
Lighting and Audiovisual Designer, Verity Hampson
Sound Designer, Jeremy Silver
Associate Lighting Designer, Daniel Barber
Stage Manager, Karina McKenzie
Videographer, Xanon Murphy

CHARACTERS

AUGUSTA MACQUARIE

AUNT OLYMPIA

BASRA

VISI/VIKA

JEFF CLEVELAND

MASKED FIGURE (who appears only via video)

The other character in this play is the turquoise elephant itself. How this character is solved, theatrically, will depend on budget, space, and directorial and design choices. It may be that the elephant appears physically on stage, or maybe its presence is only suggested by sound, by videography or by lighting. Whichever choice is made, it should mesmerise, unsettle and perhaps even frighten us a little.

Regarding the Visi/Vika doubling, note that the audience should think it is Visi throughout. They are not in on the duplicity until it is revealed in the plot. The characters are distinguished on the page to assist the actor playing the roles. The theatre program should probably only acknowledge Visi.

SETTING

The household of a powerful, wealthy family. Sometime in the near future. It is 'now' with the dial turned up.

In this version of the script, it is clearly Australia; but the point should be that this could be any first world country. The place names and cultural references can be changed to suit national context.

This play went to press before the end of rehearsals and may differ from the play as performed.

SCENE ONE

Video of a FIGURE *in an ornate decorated mask, voice moderated slightly for the purposes of disguise.*

MASKED FIGURE: We are The Cultural Front for Environmental Preservation.

We are a political art movement who decry politicians and artists who say nothing and do nothing about the survival of the planet when all around us sea levels are rising, ice is melting, forests are drying up, and species are dying on a colossal scale.

You've heard the overnight news. Sea water has entered Melbourne's sewerage system. The city has awoken to discover its underground rail system is flooding and all the government can do is stand by and wring its hands.

'Oh dear.'

'We thought this was only supposed to happen in Tuvalu.'

Meanwhile the World Business Summit convenes in Sydney.

Really?

Melbourne is quite literally drowning in its own shit, and all Sydney can do is call a Business Summit?

Ironically enough, it would appear that bullshit has been estab-lished as the currency of the talks. In response, we, The Cultural Front for Environmental Preservation, have created an ... excre-mental artwork. We call it: 'Cut the Crap—or Have it Back'.

We hope you enjoy viewing it as much as we enjoyed making it.

And suddenly we are in the lounge room of the Macquarie family. BASRA *has flicked off the video screens and is numb—frozen— with shock.*

BASRA: Melbourne? Oh, my God! But this wasn't supposed to happen for years. Decades ...

I should—

I should—

But what can BASRA *do?*

A sudden roaring gale as AUGUSTA MACQUARIE *enters, splattered head to toe in shit. Someone has clearly attempted to clean her up. She slams the door shut and locks the inferno out.*

AUGUSTA: Basra!

BASRA *is still rooted to the spot, immobilised by shock.*

Basra! Help me.

BASRA: [*coming to*] Oh God, you stink!

AUGUSTA: It's human.

BASRA: What did you do—shit in a fan?

AUGUSTA: Don't be disgusting. I need to be stripped clean and watergunned.

BASRA: You're supposed to be at the Summit.

AUGUSTA: I can't stay there like this!

BASRA: I was looking for you on TV, but all they're talking about now is what's happening in Melbourne and some artwork they—

AUGUSTA: Where's the maid?

BASRA: The Philippines.

AUGUSTA: Cecilia?

BASRA: She left on Sunday.

AUGUSTA: Not another one of those hysterical Catholic festivals.

BASRA: Her mother—

AUGUSTA: Some sighting of the Virgin Mary on a garbage mountain.

BASRA: Her family has just been wiped out by a category six typhoon.

AUGUSTA: Not again.

BASRA: They've lost everything.

AUGUSTA: When's she coming back?

BASRA: The agency's sending a replacement.

AUGUSTA: You'll have to do it.

BASRA: I'm not touching you!

AUGUSTA: Get me out of these. Incinerate them. Thank God it's summer. Can you imagine this on my stole? Jesus on a sandwich!

BASRA: What actually happened to you?

BASRA *searches for a bin liner.*

AUGUSTA: The Summit opening. Two lunatics with buckets. Flung it all over the Australian delegation. 'This is what you give us. Have some of it back.' That's what she said. The shrill one. Some kind of machine doing it to her voice. There was a shrill one and a cretin. The delegates thought it was part of the opening ceremony. People actually applauded.

BASRA: Oh, my God.

She bursts into laughter.

AUGUSTA: Have I said something funny?

BASRA: You're the artwork.

She can't stop laughing.

It was the Cultural Front, wasn't it? You're their excremental installation.

AUGUSTA: I don't want to talk about it.

BASRA: You've been Fronted. Don't touch a thing. You could be worth millions in a few years.

BASRA *assists in the clean-up throughout the following.*

AUGUSTA: 'The Front'. Trying to make themselves sound like artists, I suppose.

BASRA: They are artists. They're an internet sensation! How can you not have heard of them?

AUGUSTA: Why should I have?

BASRA: They're the ones who covered themselves in red paint and lay across the M1—remember? Brought it to a standstill for days. To protest against human trafficking. Called the work 'Road Kill'.

AUGUSTA: I'm having them listed.

BASRA: On what?

AUGUSTA: The terrorist register.

BASRA: You should be funding them, not banning them.

AUGUSTA: This isn't protest. This is animal behaviour.

BASRA: How else do they get the message through? Genius. 'Stop the Crap.'

AUGUSTA: I mean, really? *Really?* How dare they—

BASRA: Oh, they dare.

AUGUSTA: How *dare* they violate—

BASRA: They have every right to comment—

AUGUSTA: No, I'm talking, Basra. *I'm* talking.

Beat.

How *dare* they presume they have the right to desecrate another human being—

BASRA: You weren't being desecrated. You're not a holy relic.

AUGUSTA: —in such a base and—

BASRA: 'Defiled' maybe.

AUGUSTA: —and disrespectful way?

BASRA: 'Vandalised.'

AUGUSTA: Vandals. Yes, they're vandals. Not artists. Not environmentalists. Vandals.

BASRA: Haven't you seen the news?

AUGUSTA: I am the news!

BASRA: Not this morning.

AUGUSTA: I will be by dinner time.

BASRA: You have seen Melbourne? You do realise how critical things have just become?

AUGUSTA: What—the sewerage?

BASRA: The sea water has entered the sewerage system, yes.

AUGUSTA: A few suburbs—

BASRA: The entire CBD.

AUGUSTA: Don't exaggerate.

BASRA: Water. Filling the train stations.

AUGUSTA: Some temporary inundation. Honestly. What's all the fuss about?

BASRA: Everything's changed now.

AUGUSTA: What has?

BASRA: It's finally happening.

AUGUSTA: What?

BASRA: It.

The tipping point.

AUGUSTA: Yes.

And the people in a position to turn it around and do something about it are gathered in a room together in the Sofitel—strategising—while I'm stuck here rinsing faeces out of my hair.

BASRA: We should be protesting on the streets.

AUGUSTA: Go on then.

She picks up a controller, points it towards the door. Flicks the switch. The gale returns.

It's lovely outside. Forty-eight degrees in the shade. Off you pop.

A détente. Flicks the switch again.

Honestly, Basra. You live here in a dream world. What's happening out there can only be fixed by realists.

BASRA: So what exactly is it that the realists have gathered to do? Are you working on tax loopholes for big polluters? I hear there's money in sewerage treatment at the moment.

AUGUSTA: We're challenging the science on climate change once and for all. Killing it dead.

BASRA: What?

AUGUSTA: Things have gone too far. Today's events prove it.

BASRA: Oh, you think?

AUGUSTA: We've given the recyclers and wind farmers a quarter of a century to solve this. It's only gotten worse. The Green movement has failed. Worse than that. It's lied. We've found the evidence.

BASRA: Of what?

AUGUSTA: A cover-up. The Bureau of Meteorology has kept it hidden. Deliberately concealed the evidence.

BASRA: What evidence?

AUGUSTA: That this is exactly what happened before the last Ice Age.

BASRA: Not heat like this.

AUGUSTA: Yes, dear.

BASRA: It has never regularly hit fifty degrees on this continent before. Never.

AUGUSTA: How do you know?

BASRA: The Antarctic ice shelf melted in a year. It was supposed to float around for decades.

AUGUSTA: Exactly like the last time.

BASRA: That's simply not true.

AUGUSTA: Yes it is.

BASRA: Because you say so? You're making this up.

AUGUSTA: We've produced new figures.

BASRA: I bet. Where from? The TAB?

AUGUSTA: Core samples.

BASRA: Where?

AUGUSTA: The arctic tundra. A university in Murmansk. And another one in Houston.

BASRA: Oh, well, then …!

AUGUSTA: I'm heading back later this week and presenting it all in a keynote. Historical data. Cycles of warming and cooling. The patterns are there to see. It's uncanny.

BASRA: It's bullshit.

AUGUSTA: We need to go back to fossil fuels. Coal. Uranium! Now! Renewables are what got us into this mess. Solar panels are useless if we're about to plummet into another Ice Age. No sun, no power.

BASRA: That's crazy.

AUGUSTA: No, dear. Perfectly sensible.

BASRA: No, Grandma—it's actually insane. No wonder The Front targeted you.

AUGUSTA: Them? Ha! They're irrelevant. Let them target me.

>   *Beat.*

Oh, God, I just remembered: your aunt!

BASRA: Don't panic. She gets here tomorrow.

AUGUSTA: But the car—

BASRA: —will be cleaned in time. Gregor will take care of it.

AUGUSTA: The man's a saint. We need to pay him more.

BASRA: Says the Queen of the Minimum Wage.

AUGUSTA: Here.

>   *She dumps the last of her outer layers into the bin liner.*

Give them to the homeless.

>   *She's about to head off and then recalls something.*

The strangest thing happened on the drive home. I thought I saw something on the streets. An elephant.

BASRA: An elephant?

AUGUSTA: It was blue.

BASRA: What?

AUGUSTA: Or green. That colour in between.

BASRA: You saw a turquoise elephant?

AUGUSTA: I know. It's silly, isn't it? Just for a minute. Out of the corner of my eye. Then when I turned to look at it directly … it vanished.

>   *Beat.*

BASRA *is away with the pixies.* AUGUSTA *clicks her fingers in front of* BASRA's *eyes.*

Basra, really, what's wrong with you today?

BASRA: It's just that—my blog. My blog is called *The Turquoise Elephant.*

AUGUSTA: Is it?

BASRA: Of course it is. I've told you a dozen times.

AUGUSTA: I suppose I must have known that.

BASRA: It's my work.

AUGUSTA: It's a hobby, Basra.

BASRA: It's what I do. I write about climate change. And turquoise elephants. And then Melbourne floods, and you see one. On the streets.

AUGUSTA: Nonsense. I just said I *thought* I—

BASRA: It's a sign.

AUGUSTA: Of what?

BASRA: I need to …

AUGUSTA: What?

BASRA: Watch.

> I need to watch it all.
> Take it all in.
> And then …

AUGUSTA: What?

BASRA: And then I'll know what to do.

AUGUSTA *stares at her perplexedly.*

AUGUSTA: Basra?

> Have you been taking the Stillnox again?

BASRA: Yes.

> What? No.

AUGUSTA *leaves warily.*

AUGUSTA: Spray everything I've touched.

BASRA *opens up her laptop. Waits for it to reboot. Picks up the remote control and is about to turn the video screens on again when there is a buzz at the door.*

BASRA: Shit.

She presses the intercom.

You're a day early, Aunt Olympia. The driver's only just dropped Grandma off. He has to sterilise the car—

VISI: [*via the intercom*] It's Visi.

BASRA: Who?

VISI: Visi. The agency sent me.

BASRA: The—Oh! Of course. Come on up. [*To herself*] Shit, shit, shit.

> BASRA *exits and reappears with a can and sprays the air.* VISI *enters quietly.*

VISI: Do you disinfect everyone who comes in here?

BASRA: What? Oh—No. Us. I'm disinfecting us. Not you.

VISI: I don't have—

BASRA: No. My grandmother. She—

VISI: What?

BASRA: —came in covered in shit.

VISI: The agency didn't tell me that.

BASRA: It's not typical. You wouldn't normally have to—

> *Beat.* BASRA *puts the can away.*

VISI: I can come back.

BASRA: Trust me. There's never a 'right' time to enter this house.

> *Beat.*

Is it still blowing a gale out there?

VISI: The wind picks up and dies down. It's weird.

BASRA: Like a furnace. And still my grandmother insists we're heading for an Ice Age. Any day now, apparently.

I've got to do something about it.

VISI: The Ice Age?

BASRA: My grandmother. I've got to stop her.

VISI: From what?

BASRA: From talking to them.

VISI: Who?

BASRA: The World Business Council.

VISI: Stop her how?

BASRA: Phone someone. Or sign something.

VISI: Sign what?

BASRA: I said I don't know!

Beat.

I'm sorry. I've only just found out. I'm—

VISI: You're upset.

BASRA: Yes.

VISI: Okay.

Beat.

This house is like a fortress.

BASRA: Yeah right. It's just missing the cannons.

VISI: Who's the enemy?

BASRA: Not 'who'. 'What'. Check out the windows. Triple-glazed.

VISI *looks at the windows—huge floor-to-ceiling jobs that 'separate' audience and actors.*

VISI: Wow. Is this like … bulletproofing?

BASRA: Weatherproofing. An impermeable membrane between us and the rest of the planet. We have our own microclimate. You wouldn't know the Anthropocene is taking place outside.

VISI: The what?

BASRA: Climate change. Human generated.

VISI: Oh, right.

BASRA: But you'd know about that, right?

VISI: —

BASRA: You've seen what's happening in Melbourne. I don't need to lecture you about rising sea levels.

VISI: I'm not political.

BASRA: But you're alive. Living in this time and place.

A silence.

An awkward exchange of smiles.

BASRA *gestures towards a seat.* VISI *remains standing.*

So. The house is huge, but there are only three bedrooms. Mine, Grandma's—Augusta, that is. You can call her that, by the way.

VISI: Isn't it 'Your Excellency'? The agency said—

BASRA: She hasn't been Governor-General for ten years. Call her Augusta. For me. The other room is the guest room. The Serengeti Suite. Oh. My. God. You should lock yourself in there sometime. Surround sound—storms rolling in across the plains. The vents actually pump negative ions into the room. You can experience the world. Without ever having to leave this house.

VISI: Right.

BASRA: Mostly it's Aunt Olympia who stays there. She's arriving tomorrow. And I'm sorry, but this needs to be said. The cleaning can get a little … *rococo* after she's been here.

> *Beat.*

Are you sure you want to take us on?

VISI: Don't you want to see my papers?

BASRA: The agency sent you, didn't they?

VISI: Yes.

BASRA: So they've screened you.

VISI: Sure.

BASRA: They're meticulous. They've weeded out a paedophile and two voluntary euthanasia advocates already. Do you have a visa?

VISI: To where?

BASRA: Here.

VISI: This is where I live.

BASRA: Of course, I just meant are you here permanently? The last … um …

VISI: It's okay. You can say it.

BASRA: … *employee* we had here—

VISI: Servant.

BASRA: —the last *worker* left to head back to the Philippines.

VISI: What's left of it.

BASRA: Yeah, right. Is your island …

VISI: What?

BASRA: Is it … above …

VISI: Average?

BASRA: Water.

VISI: If it wasn't above water it wouldn't be an island.

BASRA: Sure. But is it okay? Your home?

> VISI *crosses to window.*

VISI: Everything looks okay. Well, aside from it being forty-eight degrees outside. And Melbourne flooding. And coming tenth at our own Olympics. In Brisbane. That was awkward. But on the whole I'd say yes, everything's fine on my island.

Pause.

BASRA: I'm sorry.

VISI: What for?

BASRA: I've made a completely racist assumption.

VISI: That I wouldn't care about the Olympics?

BASRA: I totally assumed you were here on an environmental resettlement visa. Oh, God. This is so embarrassing.

Silence.

VISI: My parents came here when their island drowned. They were environmental refugees. One of the first ones.

BASRA: I'm sorry.

Beat.

You want the job?

VISI: Are you offering it to me?

BASRA: Yes.

VISI: Yes.

I would like the job.

Thank you.

They shake hands.

TRANSITION SEQUENCE:

MASKED FIGURE: We're back. Still no action from our assembled world leaders. Mass evacuations from Melbourne; rising panic in the streets of our other capital cities; but still no action from the coal-stained fingers holding the global purse strings. What a surprise.

Oh, well, let's see if this image speaks loudly enough for you to hear.

We've just blown up the Environment Minister's car in the Sofitel lobby. Pity—it was a Prius.

We filled it with paint and called the spattered wreckage 'Melting Poles'. We like to think Pollock would have approved.

This is the final 'wake-up' call.

This morning's positive protest action was timed to avoid injury. But the time is coming, if peaceful, artistic protest is not listened to, when we will be forced to create works of art painted in human blood, not red paint.

Be warned. The Planet Murderers must be stopped.

SCENE TWO

VISI *and* BASRA *in the lounge room.* VISI *at a video recorder, while* BASRA *grandstands.*

BASRA: Tell me when you're ready.

VISI: Go.

BASRA: [*reading*] 'In the face of overwhelming global events, it's always difficult to ask what it is that the individual can do to change things. I refer specifically here to the catastrophic events taking place in our world as a result of human impact upon the environment—'

She breaks for a moment from her prepared speech.

Yes, I'm talking about climate change, and yes, I'm saying that we are responsible for what's happening in Melbourne. All of us.

Back to her notes.

[*Reading*] 'I hereby publicly announce that I am withdrawing my inheritance from all investment in fossil fuels and am reinvesting it in clean and renewable energy. Upon the death of my grandmother and great aunt, I will do the same with the remainder of our fortune. That sum will eventually represent a ten-billion-dollar redirection of resources—

VISI: [*breaking from the videoing*] Holy fuck!

BASRA: What?

VISI: You're worth ten billion?! You?!

BASRA: Well, my family has investments somewhere in that—

VISI: Ten billion?!

BASRA: I know. It's obscene.

VISI: You could fucking *buy* Melbourne.

BASRA: At the moment *you* could buy Melbourne.

VISI: And you get all that when they die? What about your parents?

BASRA: My parents are dead. Journalists. Long story. I was supposed to get the money when I was eighteen. Then twenty-one. Then twenty-five. She keeps pushing it back and back, but—I'm going to make her give it to me. Now. Today.

VISI: You don't think it's too late?

BASRA: What do you mean?

VISI: Is investing in renewables going to do what you want it to do?

BASRA: What?

VISI: Stop global warming.

BASRA: It's better than doing nothing, surely.

VISI: Okay.

BASRA: What?

VISI: Nothing.

BASRA: What?

VISI: Not to piss on your parade or anything. But. You know …

BASRA: What?

VISI: It doesn't matter.

    Beat.

BASRA: No.

    I don't think it's too late.

VISI: Okay.

    Beat.

BASRA: For someone who says they're not political you seem to have some strong opinions about the timing of the planet's demise.

    Beat.

VISI: Sorry.

    Beat.

    So what do you do?

BASRA: About what?

VISI: For a job.

BASRA: Well, I … I'm an activist, actually.

VISI: What do you mean?

BASRA: I know. Conversation killer, right?

VISI: That's a job?

BASRA: I'm a freelance writer. I submit articles. To magazines. About the environment.

VISI: So, you're a journalist too.

BASRA: An activist.

VISI: They don't get published?

BASRA: Mostly I blog. I have ten thousand followers.

VISI: So it's like a boutique thing?

BASRA: Well—

VISI: Do they pay you?

BASRA: I—That's not the point.

VISI: What's it about?

BASRA: It's hard to explain.

VISI: But your readers get it.

BASRA: I hope so.

VISI: So why wouldn't I?

BASRA: Right. Of course. It's called *The Turquoise Elephant*.

VISI: Why turquoise?

BASRA: It's the colour for the post-Green movement. The ones who want to return to Eden. Turquoise, like pristine waters. It's aspirational.

VISI: So give me an example.

BASRA: Of a turquoise elephant?

VISI: —

BASRA: Really?

Beat.

Well … I posted this photo essay. Of deckchairs and banana lounges. Floating in the Indian Ocean. They'd washed up on Christmas Island. Crashed against the rocks there. They were from the Maldives. The hotel insignia was on the back of the … the headrest of one of the cabana lounges. It's like, the Maldives have gone, and this symbol of luxury and Western tourist consumption … decadence, if you like … has washed up on this other island that is synonymous with *human* sea wrack …

Silence.

That's not offensive, is it? To you?

Beat.

VISI: That's clever.

The intercom buzzer blares.

OLYMPIA: [*off*] Augusta!

BASRA: Oh, Jesus.

OLYMPIA: [*off*] Augusta, let me in!

BASRA: Brace yourself.

OLYMPIA: [*off, regally, blaring like a foghorn*] Open the drawbridge!

VISI: You've got a drawbridge?

OLYMPIA: [*off*] Hurry up! If I don't urinate immediately I'm going to unleash the sort of deluge that hasn't been seen since Noah.

BASRA: [*to* OLYMPIA] Hang on!

OLYMPIA: [*off*] It will be biblical!

BASRA: Okay, it's open.

OLYMPIA: [*off*] Species will be extinguished.

BASRA: I said it's open.

OLYMPIA: [*off*] Starting with the ground-dwelling rodentia.

BASRA: Aunt Olympia—

OLYMPIA: [*off*] The dunnart, the dalgyte, the quokka, the quenda …

VISI: What's a 'quenda'?

BASRA: I don't know.

OLYMPIA: [*off*] Flushed from their warrens—

BASRA: *Aunt Olympia—*

OLYMPIA: [*off*] —by a warm nitric torrent—

BASRA: *—the fucking door is open!*

Beat.

OLYMPIA: [*off*] Thank you!

VISI: Wow.

BASRA: I know, right?

VISI: What was the word you used before? For the cleaning?

BASRA: Rococo?

VISI: I think I get it now.

> OLYMPIA *enters to a blast of hot wind. Quite possibly wrapped in something endangered. An ocelot, or a hat made out of some rare bird. Staggers in with leaves etc. blowing. She plonks a large, dripping plastic bag on the bench.*

OLYMPIA: Fridge.

Beat.

I'm ready to burst my banks. Nearly had to relieve myself in the car. How on earth Gregor got me through that traffic … Apparently some extremists blew up Jackson Pollock at a hotel. Where are we? Palmyra? And then before we knew it, we were swamped with itinerants! People, leaving the city in droves! Horns tooting! Tempers flaring!

BASRA: We were just looking at the footage.

OLYMPIA: Packing up their lives and strapping it to the top of their cars. You'd think there was a meteor coming.

BASRA: There is.

OLYMPIA: Who's this?

VISI: I'm Visi.

OLYMPIA: Do I know you?

VISI: No.

OLYMPIA: Help or hindrance?

VISI: What?

OLYMPIA: Are you the help or just one of her friends?

BASRA: Visi's working for us now.

OLYMPIA: Right, then. Point me straight to the nearest commode.

BASRA: You know where it is.

OLYMPIA: Where's Augusta?

BASRA: In her bunker. Writing a Nazi war speech.

OLYMPIA: Where am I bivouacked?

BASRA: The Serengeti …

OLYMPIA: If I don't expire from dehydration along the way. It's forty-eight degrees outside. [*To* VISI] Cart the portmanteau, will you?

She heads down the hall.

Forty-eight degrees! Honestly. It's worse than Bombay.

VISI: Is that where she's been?

BASRA: Just now? No. Greenland. To see the last of the permafrost melting. She's part of this group. These vampires who tour the world to witness environmental collapse. Like storm chasers or whatnot. Those tornado freaks? They try to chase these moments of cataclysm.

The exact moment the ice shelf falls into the sea. Or the last fucking polar bear drowns or whatever. Ghoulish, right?

VISI: What's in the bag?

They peer in.

BASRA: Oh, God, it's dripping blood.

VISI: Meat.

BASRA: It's defrosted in the—

VISI: There's half a cow in there.

BASRA: [*starting to laugh hysterically*] You must think we're this … Chamber of Horrors.

VISI *lugs the port off.* AUGUSTA *enters.*

AUGUSTA: Was that racket Olympia arriving?

BASRA: Yes.

AUGUSTA: Have Visi make some tea. Call me when it's ready. This speech won't write itself.

BASRA: You're serious about this? You're really going ahead with it?

AUGUSTA: Of course.

BASRA: So, you make this keynote telling the world to go back to fossil fuels—killing off thirty years of advancements in renewables—and then what?

AUGUSTA: And then we follow through.

BASRA: How?

AUGUSTA: We make a resolution, as a peak global body—a treaty—and then we take it to parliament the next time it sits. We ask our government to be the first in the world to ratify the treaty. Then the world follows suit. It all begins with us. Actions, you see. Words first, and then action.

BASRA: I want my inheritance.

AUGUSTA: What for?

BASRA: I'm channelling it into renewables.

AUGUSTA: Oh, no. No, no, no, no.

BASRA: Just my share of it!

VISI *re-enters and stands silently.*

AUGUSTA: Never.

BASRA: It's my money!

AUGUSTA: It's family money. As fast as I can invest it, Olympia fritters it away on expensive indulgences and fripperies. I'm not letting you waste it too.

BASRA: It's as much mine as yours.

AUGUSTA: You can't be trusted.

BASRA: Daddy would want me to have it.

AUGUSTA: Then he should have died with a will. Gallivanting from war zone to war zone. Pouring money into lost causes. Can you imagine? You would have been as bad as him. No-one under forty should be entrusted with inherited wealth.

BASRA: But—

AUGUSTA: I've said no, and I mean no. Don't ask me again. And don't ever use Duncan as emotional leverage. He is off limits.

She exits imperiously.

A humiliated silence.

VISI: Should I—

Indicates the recording equipment.

BASRA: Pack it up.

VISI: Do you want me to download the—

BASRA: Delete it.
Trash it.
Burn it.
I don't care.
Throw the fucking thing away.

VISI *quietly packs it up and puts it away.*

VISI: You shouldn't be disheartened.
The blog.
It's good.
It's doing something.

BASRA: Something inconsequential.

VISI: You write well.

Beat.

BASRA: Thank you.

AUGUSTA *and* OLYMPIA *swan in together, washed and toileted.*

OLYMPIA: Sweet relief!

AUGUSTA: I need a drink.

OLYMPIA: A tea party!

AUGUSTA: Yes, a cleansing tisane.

VISI: [*to* BASRA] What's a tisane?

OLYMPIA: Clean cups!

AUGUSTA: Visi, do you have that tea made?

OLYMPIA: Clean plates!

AUGUSTA: Be quiet, Olympia.

VISI: What tea?

AUGUSTA: Excuse me?

BASRA: I didn't ask her to do it.

OLYMPIA: Are there biscuits?

AUGUSTA: Well, do it now.

OLYMPIA: I said, *'Are there biscuits?!'*

AUGUSTA: Stop shouting, Olympia!

OLYMPIA: What?

AUGUSTA: [*gesturing*] Turn. On. Your. Cochlear.

VISI: I'm sorry. I'll just—

OLYMPIA: Oh! There we are.

BASRA: Don't lift a finger.

OLYMPIA: Flick of a switch.

BASRA: I'll make it.

VISI: No, I'll do it.

AUGUSTA: Honestly, girl, it should be automatic. We shouldn't have to ask. Have you worked for a family like ours before?

> VISI *stares blankly at her.*

Government service, I mean.

VISI: I cleaned for a High Court judge.

AUGUSTA: Oh, well. Near enough. You should know better.

VISI: Yes, Augus—Your Excellency.

> BASRA *and* VISI *attend to the tea and biscuits together.*

OLYMPIA: This is the cochlear you got me for Christmas, Augusta. For the theatre. The one that edits out vulgarisms. You got it so I didn't have to listen to all the swear words in the new plays, remember? I only go to the classics now. Just in case. I mean, really, why bother?

It's all been said before, hasn't it? I think probably there's nothing original left to say.

BASRA: [*to* VISI] One of them doesn't hear anything she doesn't want to, the other one doesn't see it.

AUGUSTA: What does that make you? The one that doesn't say anything original?

OLYMPIA: Hear no evil, see no evil …

BASRA: Oh, that's me. The family mute.

OLYMPIA: We're all monkeys. You've arrived at feeding time, Cissy.

>OLYMPIA *screeches like a monkey.*

>*A buzzer goes off. Like one of those contraptions at restaurants that tell you your meal's ready.*

AUGUSTA: What's on earth's that din?

OLYMPIA: I'm a macaque!

AUGUSTA: Not that—the buzzing.

OLYMPIA: Oh! It's me!

>*She reads the contraption.*

It's Kilimanjaro!

AUGUSTA: What about it?

OLYMPIA: The last of the snow is melting.

AUGUSTA: Right now?

OLYMPIA: Forever. Oh, that would be fabulous to see.

AUGUSTA: Then go.

OLYMPIA: But I only just got back. I think I'll click 'no'. Although Jeff might be going …

AUGUSTA: Oh, for God's sake, make up your mind, woman.

OLYMPIA: Do I stay or do I go?

AUGUSTA: You're becoming existential, Olympia.

OLYMPIA: I think I'll stay.

>*Clicks the button.*

BASRA: Seen one snow melt, seen them all.

OLYMPIA: Mind you, I'm quite annoyed about missing Melbourne.

BASRA: Rude of them not to schedule that for your entertainment.

OLYMPIA: Yes. Oh, well. New Orleans was better. Now! Let me tell you about Greenland. I saw it, you know!

AUGUSTA: What?

OLYMPIA: The musk ox.

AUGUSTA: There's no such thing.

OLYMPIA: Of course there is.

AUGUSTA: They became extinct years ago.

OLYMPIA: I don't think so, dear.

AUGUSTA: Yes. There are no musk ox left.

OLYMPIA: I saw one, dear.

AUGUSTA: And if there was there wouldn't be any in Greenland.

OLYMPIA: There are now. In the savannah plains. Magnificent!

AUGUSTA: You were hallucinating, Olympia.

OLYMPIA: Well, it was a collective hallucination in that case. That's what's in the bag.

Everyone stares at it.

BASRA: That—carcass—is a musk ox?

OLYMPIA: Yes.

BASRA: How did you get it through customs?

OLYMPIA: Oh, we don't worry about that. It's dinner.

BASRA/AUGUSTA/VISI: Dinner?

OLYMPIA: Yes. I only eat endangered species now.

BASRA: That's revolting.

OLYMPIA: That's how you save the species.

BASRA: By eating it?

OLYMPIA: Yes! Supply and demand.

AUGUSTA: Ah—the free market.

OLYMPIA: They're being commercially farmed.

AUGUSTA: The free market prevails! You see? Not governments. Not environmental fanatics!

OLYMPIA: Farmers.

AUGUSTA: I think that's marvellous.

BASRA: It's macabre.

AUGUSTA: You don't live in the real world, Basra. Never have.

VISI: How do you cook it?

OLYMPIA: Curry it. Twelve hours, apparently. To break down the muscle and sinew. A few cloves and spices. You'll know what to do with it. You are the cook, aren't you?

Pause.

VISI: Yes, I'm the cook.

OLYMPIA: Wonderful! Thank you, Cissy.

BASRA: It's Visi.

VISI *hauls it off.*

BASRA *pours the tea. Hands a cup to* OLYMPIA.

OLYMPIA: Now. I need to tell you. I met someone. On the ship, and—

AUGUSTA: What do you mean you 'met' someone?

OLYMPIA: An odd sort. But he found me fascinating.

BASRA: Was he a psychiatrist?

OLYMPIA: No, a tycoon. Made all his money in microchips and nano something-or-other. Kept blathering on about 'The Paradigm'. 'The Paradigm' this and 'The Paradigm' that.

BASRA: What paradigm exactly?

OLYMPIA: I don't know. But he was *exhausted* by 'The Paradigm' and was 'Going Inside'.

AUGUSTA: Inside where? Not you, I hope.

OLYMPIA: Australia. To the outback. He's set his sights on this enormous cattle run that he wants to convert.

BASRA: To what?

OLYMPIA: To a paradise. The Hanging Gardens of Carpentaria. Tens of thousands of square kilometres. Half the country. Under a dome. A new world.

BASRA: Like a utopia?

OLYMPIA: I suppose so. I didn't understand most of it. But he was clearly obsessed.

AUGUSTA: He's after your money, Olympia.

OLYMPIA: He has money, Augusta.

AUGUSTA: Then why was he interested in you?

OLYMPIA: Oh, there was some other harpy trying to get her hooks into him. You know the type. Some gaping-mouthed acolyte. One of the women who wear amber. But I tell you his eyes were on me the whole trip.

BASRA: Where is this settlement exactly?

AUGUSTA: Yes, why haven't I heard of it?

OLYMPIA: All a big secret. He's searching for pilgrims.

AUGUSTA: There are more of them?

OLYMPIA: Somewhere. All boarding the ark together.

AUGUSTA: And warning bells didn't start ringing then?

OLYMPIA: Preserving the human race.

BASRA: Sounds fascinating.

OLYMPIA: The animals marched on two by two. Now there's a retirement plan for us, Augusta.

AUGUSTA: I don't do retirement.

OLYMPIA: I suspect he wants me to join him.

AUGUSTA: Oh, God. It's a doomsday cult. Stay away, Olympia.

OLYMPIA: 'New Eden' they're calling it.

BASRA: No, seriously, this sounds really interesting. Has anyone else written about this?

OLYMPIA: I told you—it's a secret.

BASRA: What's his name?

OLYMPIA: Jeff.

AUGUSTA: Of course it is.

BASRA: Would he be available for interview, do you think?

AUGUSTA: Don't tell her any more, Olympia.

BASRA: How would I contact him?

OLYMPIA: You won't have to.

AUGUSTA: Thank you.

OLYMPIA: He's coming here.

AUGUSTA: He's what?

OLYMPIA: On his way to New Eden. I've invited him here to stay.

Beat.

Well, don't look at me like that. There's plenty of room in the Serengeti.

TRANSITION SEQUENCE:

The MASKED FIGURE*'s tone has now shifted from one of cultured, lofty detachment to something more urgent. There are elements of zeal sneaking in.*

MASKED FIGURE: Three days of aching tedium at this indulgent global yack-fest, and still no action. The first cases of cholera have broken out in Melbourne. People are abandoning the city in their hundreds of thousands and forming makeshift camps all over the country. The Australian continent is now witnessing its largest mass migration since the last Ice Age. What is it going to take to convince you people that drastic action is needed and it's needed now?!

A little bird has told us that our wealthy summiteers are working on a treaty. They are about to propose a return to fossil fuels as a solution to the environmental apocalypse that is unfolding around us.

Well, here's a counterproposal for you: if this purported treaty makes the light of day, the next image you see filling your screens will be one of carnage. Art and life will merge in a single terrifying moment of creativity.

You won't be able to look away.

A sudden, staticky jump cut to silence. Suddenly we are back inside the domestic scene.

SCENE THREE

VIKA—*though of course we think it is still* VISI—*is doing* AUGUSTA*'s hair. Some kind of bouffant ridiculousness.* OLYMPIA *is 'eating' the musk ox curry. She chews and chews the meat to absorb its flavour and then spits the food matter into an ostentatious spittoon.* AUGUSTA *and* VISI *brace in unison with each spit.*

OLYMPIA: Where's Basra?

AUGUSTA: Blogging.

OLYMPIA: In her bedroom? Sounds revolting. The word itself—reeks of disgorgement. I might get my cochlear to edit it out. What's it called again?

AUGUSTA: What?

OLYMPIA: The girl's blog.

AUGUSTA: *The Turquoise Elephant.*

OLYMPIA: Sounds pretty. Like something you might encounter through the looking glass. Turquoise. Hm.

   Spit.

I might invent a colour. Before I die. And that will be my politic. Heliotrope!

AUGUSTA: Already invented.

OLYMPIA: That's my favourite *word* for a colour. 'She enters in helio-trope and diamonds.' That's Wilde, isn't it? Oscar Wilde?

AUGUSTA: I don't know, Olympia.

OLYMPIA: 'Heliotrope'. Just saying it. Feels somehow … erotic.

    VIKA *pulls too tightly on* AUGUSTA*'s hair.*

AUGUSTA: Ow!

VIKA: Sorry.

OLYMPIA: You there. Vicky.

VIKA: [*simultaneously*] Vika.

AUGUSTA: [*simultaneously*] Visi.

VIKA: [*quickly correcting herself*] Visi. My family call me Vika. But it's Visi.

OLYMPIA: You've been silent all morning. Wise choice. I never speak unless I have something fascinating to say. For instance: I read this week that that we're attracted to the scent of people with the same political beliefs as us.

    Beat.

Isn't that fascinating? If the reverse is true, then those whose views we oppose must reek.

    BASRA *enters with a laptop.*

BASRA: We're taking in two refugee families.

AUGUSTA: We're what?

BASRA: From Melbourne.

AUGUSTA: Don't be preposterous.

BASRA: You mocked me for being passive. This is me taking action.

OLYMPIA: I thought she was busy blogging.

AUGUSTA: It's not action, Basra. It's reaction.

BASRA: The current Governor-General doesn't seem to think so.

AUGUSTA: The current Governor-General is a weak-minded fool. I have it on the best authority he's about to stand down.

BASRA: To protest his own government's inaction!

AUGUSTA: He's a fool.

BASRA: He's brilliant.

AUGUSTA: He's history.

BASRA: He's asking every family in the country to take someone in.

AUGUSTA: So it's not even your own idea.

BASRA: It's appalling that we should just sit here doing nothing while the world tilts into chaos. Stuck in this fishbowl. Watching it all unfold from the windows—on the video screens. I've made up my mind. We're helping these people.

Another spit from OLYMPIA.

AUGUSTA: Where will they stay?

BASRA: I'm giving them the winter lodge—in Jindabyne.

AUGUSTA: You can't.

BASRA: I can.

OLYMPIA: It hasn't snowed there in years. Let them have it.

BASRA: You won't give me my money, but you can't stop me handing over property I own.

AUGUSTA: We know nothing about them. They could be terrorists.

BASRA: Don't be ridiculous.

AUGUSTA: That's how they work. They infiltrate the system and take advantage.

BASRA: That is blatant prejudice and you know it.

AUGUSTA: I know how these things work, Basra.

BASRA: Too late.

AUGUSTA: I forbid it!

BASRA raises her finger over the laptop keyboard.

Don't you dare.

A click of a button.

BASRA: … and done.

AUGUSTA: You'll regret this, Basra. It will come back to bite you.

OLYMPIA *regurgitates another mouthful into the spittoon.*

BASRA: I'm sorry, but that is just disgusting. Can you please go somewhere else and do that?

OLYMPIA: Where?

BASRA: A toilet?

OLYMPIA: I haven't defecated in eighteen years.

AUGUSTA: Oh, really, Olympia. This is too much!

OLYMPIA: Not since that dreadful wog I picked up in Zanzibar.

BASRA: I can't be in the same room as this. Somebody call me when the
  visitor arrives.
OLYMPIA: Do you remember, Augusta?
AUGUSTA: No.
BASRA: Somebody?
OLYMPIA: You were there.
BASRA: Anybody?
OLYMPIA: In the Stone Town. The old slave markets.

> VIKA *catches* BASRA*'s eye and nods.* BASRA *exits.*

My *God*, the things that came out of my bowels! Fingernails. Bits of
cork. An old typewriter key. A small coin no longer in circulation.
Now how did that get there? I must have swallowed it when I was a
child. It was like I was evacuating a lifetime's bric-a-brac.
AUGUSTA: Olympia!
OLYMPIA: And then it was empty! The end. The last time I ate—or
  passed—solids. Funny, isn't it … waste. Yes …
VIKA: [*to* AUGUSTA] You're done.
AUGUSTA: Splendid. What do you think, Olympia?
OLYMPIA: Divine. You look like Boadicea.
AUGUSTA: Now all I need is the suit of armour to match. Into battle!
OLYMPIA: Into the fray!
AUGUSTA: This is perfect for tomorrow, Visi, thank you. Can you set it
  again in the morning?
VIKA: Should I come with you?
AUGUSTA: Where, dear?
VIKA: To your speech? To finish you off?
AUGUSTA: I don't think that will be necessary, dear.

> *The intercom buzzer sounds. Everyone jumps.*

OLYMPIA: That's him! He's here!
AUGUSTA: Calm down, Olympia. Screeching like a macaw. Visi, quick.
  Go and make sure all of Olympia's belongings have been shifted to
  my room.

> AUGUSTA *exits.*

JEFF: [*over the intercom*] Hello.
OLYMPIA: Yoo hoo!

AUGUSTA: There'll be no fornicating in the Rift Valley while I'm still sentient.

> BASRA *enters.*

You might need to go and help him, Basra. He may have trouble with the stairs.

OLYMPIA: Come through, the drawbridge is lowered!

AUGUSTA: I must get those handrails installed in the bathroom.

> *And* JEFF *springs into the room. A Richard Branson type. Or a Paul Theroux in his prime. An overnight bag and briefcase. Altogether younger and more corporate than what we were expecting.*

JEFF: Hello, ladies!

AUGUSTA: Oh.

OLYMPIA: Jeff.

JEFF: Miss Olympia Macquarie.

> *A long, uncomfortable kiss.*

OLYMPIA: [*flustered*] Well, now. The old engine still seems to be running.

JEFF: [*to* AUGUSTA] You must be Her Excellency.

> *A handshake.* AUGUSTA *covers her nose and mouth as he approaches, like he reeks to the heavens.*

AUGUSTA: You're about fifty years younger than we were expecting.

JEFF: Happy to surprise. [*To* BASRA] And you … My Lord. Your aunt's description didn't do you justice at all.

BASRA: Likewise.

> *A kiss of the hand.* VIKA *enters.*

JEFF: And, hello. What have we here?

OLYMPIA: The help.

JEFF: Well, well, well—aren't you a marvel? Jeff Cleveland.

VIKA: Visi.

JEFF: Visi. Beautiful. Visi and Basra. Olympia and Augusta. Have I just stumbled into the final set of a beauty pageant? Where've you got Miss Venezuela hidden?

AUGUSTA: You need a shower. You smell awful.

OLYMPIA: Pheromones.

JEFF: I choose not to bathe in artificial or treated water.

AUGUSTA: What a surprise. Visi—take his things to the Serengeti. [*Privately*] Disinfect them.

>VIKA *doesn't seem to know what to do with* JEFF*'s things.*

VIKA: What do you mean 'Take them to the Serengeti'?
JEFF: The Serengeti's where I just came from.
AUGUSTA: His room.
VIKA: I don't get it.
JEFF: Either do I.
AUGUSTA: Take them to his room.
BASRA: She means the Serengeti Suite.

>VIKA *exits, a tad warily.*

AUGUSTA: I don't think geography is her strong suit. Just as well she can set hair.
BASRA: Have a seat, Jeff. You must be exhausted.
JEFF: Oh, I slept on the plane, Miss Macquarie.
BASRA: Basra.
JEFF: Basra. Like the city on the Silk Trail?
BASRA: It's where I was conceived, I believe.
JEFF: Then I guess you should call me 'El Paso'! Ha! I just came from Kilimanjaro. The last snow on the African continent. Gone yesterday afternoon.
BASRA: I heard about it.
JEFF: Gone forever.
OLYMPIA: That would have been good to see. I should have gone too.
JEFF: You can't be in all places at once, Miss Olympia. You have to be strategic about the causes you invest in.
AUGUSTA: Olympia doesn't invest. She's just a tourist.
OLYMPIA: I'm an adventuress.
AUGUSTA: And what are you, exactly, Mr Cleveland?
JEFF: I was a nanotechnologist. An inventor.
AUGUSTA: Oh, yes. What did you invent?
JEFF: A microchip.
AUGUSTA: Which one?
BASRA: Grandma!
OLYMPIA: Did it have name?
JEFF: Now I'm a futurist.

AUGUSTA: And what future do you see yourself sharing with Olympia, precisely?

BASRA: Jesus, Grandma. Back off!

JEFF: It's okay, Basra. She's protecting her sister. I wouldn't have it any other way.

VIKA *re-enters with* JEFF*'s bag still in her hand.*

VIKA: I'm sorry—I didn't know where to put them.

BASRA: Down the hall. First door on the left.

VIKA *exits again.*

AUGUSTA: Really, what is wrong with everyone today?

JEFF: I know, right? It's crazy outside. The cars on the freeway. Where's everyone going?

BASRA: To the mountains.

AUGUSTA: Sheep.

OLYMPIA: Mountain goats.

JEFF: Cleaner air?

BASRA: Cooler weather. And fear that what's happening in Melbourne will happen here.

AUGUSTA: Ridiculous. They're built in a basin. There's no comparison.

JEFF: Pilgrims.

BASRA: Migrants.

AUGUSTA: Bolters.

JEFF: Where are they going to stay?

BASRA: Well, that's exactly what I was hoping to ask you, actually.

JEFF: What are they going to feed on?

BASRA: No-one's thinking that far in advance.

JEFF: Nobody has a plan. That's half the world's problem. Nobody. Has. A Plan.

He leaps onto the couch. VIKA *re-enters.*

Nobody has a fucking plan!

AUGUSTA: Can you take your feet off the—

JEFF: We need a plan, ladies!

Who wants to hear about the plan?

Who wants to hear about the plan from the man?

AUGUSTA: Visi—fetch me a Panadol.

JEFF: Now, here's what we're gonna do.

TRANSITION SEQUENCE:

MASKED FIGURE: Tick, tick, tick, tick.

Twelve hours to go, people.

Your governor-general's just resigned!

The wheels of government are falling off!

And now guess what—everyone's seeing elephants. Blue elephants—teal-coloured elephants—turquoise elephants. Massive hallucinations, a collective psychic response to tragedy.

Everyone's going cray-cray.

The system is falling apart and those in power stand by doing nothing.

We warned you what would happen if you didn't listen.

This is your last chance, before a work of art so indelible, you'll never forget it.

Stop the talks. Abandon the treaty.

Or *boom*!

SCENE FOUR

The living room. BASRA *and* JEFF, *with* VISI *cleaning in the background, listening.*

JEFF: You write so beautifully, Basra.

BASRA: Thank you.

JEFF: I've been following your blog.

BASRA: Since when? Last night?

JEFF: No—I've been following it for months.

BASRA: Really?

JEFF: Really.

BASRA: No!

JEFF: Yes.

BASRA: You're lying.

JEFF: I'm not! You have some great things to say. And your elephant is such a terrific metaphor for what's happening in the world.

BASRA: How so?

JEFF: It's 'the elephant in the room', right? It's what we all know is happening, but won't acknowledge. Is it real? Is it imagined? Though you and I and ninety-nine per cent of the planet know of course that it's real. It's always the one per cent we're dealing with, isn't it? Always the one per cent who stand in the way.

BASRA: It's the one per cent who own everything.

JEFF: Right.

BASRA: Who control the resources.

JEFF: Right.

BASRA: Who have the ear of government.

JEFF: You got it. And here you are. Beautiful Basra. Sitting right next to that one per cent—within sniffing distance of it. So close you can taste it. I don't think you even realise how powerful you are.

BASRA: If you're talking about my family's wealth—

JEFF: Your family's proximity to power. Your grandmother with one foot in government.

BASRA: Ears and feet? I think we're mixing our metaphors.

JEFF: And you in such an incredible position to influence …

BASRA: Oh, my grandmother doesn't listen to me.

JEFF: She should read your blog. Then she'd listen.

> *A pause as he gazes at her. She gazes back.* VISI *rolls her eyes. Coughs.*

VISI: Should I start on lunch?

BASRA: I'm not hungry.

JEFF: I'm fine.

BASRA: Maybe check on Aunt Olympia. She asked us to wake her by noon.

> VISI *exits.*

JEFF: The one per cent. I want to flip it.

BASRA: What do you mean?

JEFF: If one per cent of the population can run the world at the present time, then surely one per cent can save it too.

BASRA: Not the same one per cent.

JEFF: Right. I'm finding the other one per cent. The best. The brightest. Saving them and starting from scratch.

BASRA: Only saving one per cent?

JEFF: Hey—you gotta start somewhere. We'll start there and gradually rebuild. Like that seed bank they got buried in the ice in Norway. Store away enough of humanity to see it through the apocalypse and then kick things off afresh!

BASRA: But you'd save as many people as you could in the first instance, right?

JEFF: Sure. Aim big, right? This dome is gonna be huge!

BASRA: So conceivably you could take hundreds of refugees.

JEFF: Conceivably I could take thousands. Once we've become self-sustaining.

BASRA: When do you get underway?

JEFF: The deed of sale is sitting on some minister's desk right now. Some fine print about foreign ownership to be signed off on. Everything's in limbo until you find a new Grand Poobah to replace the one that resigned. Things should move quickly once that happens. If you've got money to burn, you should think about investing. Being part of the one per cent. Having a say in who survives. You'd be in an incredible position to do something positive.

BASRA: I'm tempted. Very tempted.

JEFF: I hope so.

VISI *enters with* OLYMPIA.

VISI: She was already up.

OLYMPIA: Doing my eurhythmics.

JEFF: Your what?

OLYMPIA: Calisthenics. Very good for the pelvic floor.

JEFF: Well now …

BASRA: Jeff was just selling me on New Eden.

VISI *snorts.*

He's saving the one per cent.

JEFF: In order to save the ninety-nine.

OLYMPIA: Yes, I know all about that. He needs builders.

JEFF: And planters. And scientists. And artists.

BASRA: So you're not taking everyone; just those with particular skills or characteristics?

JEFF: To begin with. Then we build. We rebuild humanity from the ground up.

VISI: But humanity's not gone.

JEFF: Not yet.

VISI: There are seven billion people out there …

JEFF: The great cull has begun, Visi. The paradigm's shutting down. We're about to see mass extinctions the likes of which you can't imagine. Basra—how many die in Melbourne if this cholera outbreak takes hold?

BASRA: I don't know. Hundreds?

JEFF: You think thousands won't die because it's a First World city? You think you're inured?

BASRA: Well—no, but—

JEFF: Imagine the same thing happening in Dhaka. In Kolkata. In Cairo. In LA. No-one saw Melbourne coming. It wasn't even on the radar. You mark my words—now that this ball has started rolling, it ain't gonna stop. We'll see half a billion dead within two years. Less. The timing is urgent. We've gotta get in and save them first. Starting with you, Basra. And Miss Olympia here. And Visi too, if she cares to join us.

VISI: Oh. You're looking for cleaners too?

OLYMPIA: So many disasters! I won't know where to visit first. Should we go to Cairo, Jeff?

JEFF: Not today, Miss Olympia.

OLYMPIA: I'd like to see the Sphinx submerge.

> AUGUSTA *sweeps into the room, dressed to the nines, preparing for her big speech.*

AUGUSTA: I'm stepping into the breach!

BASRA: What breach?

AUGUSTA: Interim Governor-General. Until they find a permanent replacement.

JEFF: Well, now … congratulations, your worship!

AUGUSTA: A steady hand to steer the ship.

BASRA: I don't believe it.

AUGUSTA: Believe it. I have the ear of government.

JEFF: Well now …

OLYMPIA: I hope they have their cochlear switched on.

AUGUSTA: Oh, they'll listen to me. Hands back firmly on the wheel …

JEFF: The hand that signed the paper …

BASRA: It's rigged. This isn't fair. It's all rigged!

AUGUSTA: I can't find my cameo brooch. Where is it?

BASRA: I don't know. I don't care.

AUGUSTA: I always wear it for important speeches. It's like a talisman.

OLYMPIA: Might have been stolen by the help.

AUGUSTA: I've turned the bedroom upside down.

VISI: Did you leave it in the car?

AUGUSTA: On Monday—when Gregor drove me back from the—yes. That must be it. Visi dear, you're a genius! Now get my purse. I need my contact lenses for the autocue.

> VISI *exits.*

Are you ready, Olympia?

OLYMPIA: Of course.

AUGUSTA: Basra? You haven't changed.

BASRA: You really think I want to witness this?

AUGUSTA: It would be nice to have some support in the room.

BASRA: Don't look at me. I think what you're doing is disgraceful.

AUGUSTA: Right. Stay at home. Sit here—mutely—and judge.

BASRA: I won't be sitting here mutely.

AUGUSTA: Blogging, then. Tweeting in responses. The armchair critic.

BASRA: I'm helping Jeff. I'm investing in New Eden.

JEFF: Huzzah!

AUGUSTA: With your pocket money?

BASRA: We're saving humanity. Here. From the lounge room.

AUGUSTA: That's nice, dear.

JEFF: That's great news, Basra. I'm so glad.

VISI: [*re-entering*] I've found the cameo.

BASRA: [*to* AUGUSTA] What you're about to do is evil.

AUGUSTA: Thank you, dear.

> VISI *pins the brooch to* AUGUSTA*'s dress.*

JEFF: What's she doing? Bombing China?

BASRA: Effectively.

OLYMPIA: One wants to save the planet and one wants to destroy it, but I don't know which is which.

BASRA: It's her. She wants to destroy it.

AUGUSTA: Don't misrepresent me.

BASRA: Do you want to look Visi in the eye and tell her climate change isn't happening? That her parents' island never actually disappeared at all?

AUGUSTA: I didn't say the climate isn't changing—we all know that— it's irrefutable. But I refuse to be held responsible—either personally or as a species—for the sun's natural warming and cooling cycles.

BASRA: Why not? In case you have to pay.

AUGUSTA: Don't ask questions and then answer them, Basra. It's passive aggressive.

BASRA: So is climate change denial.

AUGUSTA: Mark my words—the next Ice Age will be upon us before we know it and we'll be completely ill-prepared!

OLYMPIA: I think this is a grand time to be living in. An operatic age! To be alive to witness such spectacular adjustment. Change like this only occurs every ten or twenty thousand years. Can you imagine being there the moment Uluru emerged from a drying sea? Or the moment the Atlantic broke past Gibraltar and flooded the great Mediterranean Valley? My God! Such transcendent chaos! It's the only thing worth living for. Everything else is moribund. People bore me. Humanity hasn't had a fresh idea since the invention of the computer. But a planet arching and kicking in turmoil—grasping to survive. There's a tragic beauty in that.

BASRA: If humanity's so boring, you decadent old ghoul, why don't you just curl up and die!?

OLYMPIA: Well!

AUGUSTA: It's over, Basra. Time to concede defeat. The pragmatists are taking over: Game, set and match!

> JEFF *stands and applauds.*

JEFF: Oh, ladies, ladies. That was brilliant! Come on, Visi. Stand and give them a hand.

OLYMPIA: Who won?

JEFF: We might have to consult a video referee on a couple of those last points. But sadly, Basra, I think I'm going to have to award this one to your grandmother.

BASRA: You what?

JEFF: Oh, you won the moral argument hands down, but Her Eminence is right. We are truly in the end of days—the final stages of this phase of Earth's existence.

AUGUSTA: That's not what I said.

JEFF: It's too late to save the planet now. It's fucked. Renewables aren't going to do a damned thing to reverse this damage.

AUGUSTA: Thank you!

JEFF: But frankly, neither is uranium or coal. And I don't know that we're heading for another Ice Age necessarily, but we're plunging into some sort of apocalypse. And you and I and Miss Olympia and Visi here—all of us—are the descendants of the survivors of that last mass extinction event. Survival is in our DNA. Natural selection. That's the process I'm interested in. I'm selecting the survivors and taking them to paradise and we are starting again. The smartest, the most ingenious—

VISI: [*to herself*] The richest.

JEFF: And the most attractive. Miss Visi has finally joined in our conversation. Seems to me, ladies, that between you, you have all bases covered. Who's coming aboard?

AUGUSTA: I'd rather stick a knife in a toaster.

JEFF: Who's joining the Great Migration?

BASRA: I am.

AUGUSTA: What?

BASRA: I'm going with Jeff. I'm going to help him build New Eden.

AUGUSTA: Nonsense. I forbid it.

BASRA: I don't care.

AUGUSTA: You'll never leave the house.

BASRA: Yes, I will. When the time comes.

OLYMPIA: I'm coming too.

BASRA: I'll leave this room.

OLYMPIA: I don't know what I'm going to do there, but it's nice to be asked.

BASRA: I'll walk out the door and I'll never come back!

OLYMPIA: I think I might be a concubine.

BASRA: When the time comes.

JEFF: And what about you, Visi?

VISI *is looking out the window.*

Are you coming with us?

The faint sound of a crowd chanting.

You'll be the most beautiful woman in New Eden.

BASRA: What's that sound?

OLYMPIA: Did he just call her the most beautiful?

JEFF: It's the sound of inertia. Dying.

BASRA: Is it coming from outside?

OLYMPIA: I thought I was the most beautiful.

JEFF: It's the sound of the paradigm shutting down! Oh, holy day!

He leaps up onto the table.

The world's turning upside down!

AUGUSTA: Get off that table!

JEFF: It's time to shift the fucking, furniture, people!

It's time to pack up and leave!

The chanting gets louder. JEFF, *an ecstatic messiah. A window smashes.*

VISI: You need to take a look outside.

Half of Melbourne's sitting on your doorstep.

They all rush to the window.

AUGUSTA: Is it me? Are they protesting against me?

BASRA: They're protesting against the summit.

OLYMPIA: Who told them where we live?

AUGUSTA: Peasants.

BASRA: There are turquoise elephants—on their placards.

OLYMPIA: What are they all looking at?

BASRA: They've become a symbol.

JEFF: It's the end of days, folks, the end of days!

BASRA: Or maybe it's me.

OLYMPIA: Are we leaving?

BASRA: Maybe they're protesting against me, too.

AUGUSTA: Yes.

BASRA: Oh, my God.

OLYMPIA: What's the noise?

BASRA: Have I become the enemy?

AUGUSTA: You shouldn't have bragged so wantonly on that silly blog about housing refugees in Jindabyne!

BASRA: I didn't.

AUGUSTA: I told you that would backfire!

VISI: It made them angry. That someone worth ten billion dollars would only house two families.

BASRA: But I never bragged—I never posted that. We recorded it and I told you to throw it away.

VISI: …

JEFF: Honey, even I read it. That's what prompted me to come visit.

BASRA: The money?

OLYMPIA: No, no, you came for me.

JEFF: Of course I did, pumpkin. [*Laughing*] After I met the fascinating Miss Olympia on the cruise ship, I became interested in the whole family. She told me so much about you. I was drawn here by a young woman with such passionate principles and hopes for a better future, even in the face of global destruction. And I wasn't disappointed.

BASRA: [*to* VISI] You posted it? Why? Why would you do that?

BASRA *looks at* VISI *in disbelief. The chanting outside gets louder.*

AUGUSTA: Enough natter. Come, Visi. Forward ho! Into the tumult!

Beat.

VISI: You—you want me there?

AUGUSTA: I keep forgetting things.

VISI: Are you sure?

AUGUSTA: I need you to keep me organised.

VISI: I can't—

AUGUSTA: You asked to come the other day.

VISI: I'd have to swap.

AUGUSTA: Swap?

VISI: Change. I'm not dressed properly.

AUGUSTA: Where do you live?

VISI: It's on the way.

AUGUSTA: We don't have time.

VISI: It's near the city. I have to call them—

AUGUSTA: Well, hurry up.

VISI *stares at her for a moment. Beat. She fumbles with a mobile phone, leaves the room.*

OLYMPIA: What a dreadful noise. I think I'll shut it off.

JEFF: You need to listen to it, my friend; it's the sound of the world turning on its axis.

The ruckus swells and crescendos and turns into applause. It fills the room.

SCENE FIVE

A spotlight. AUGUSTA *walks into the limelight, arms outstretched to receive the glory in Eva Peron style. She exults in the moment.*

AUGUSTA: They say all the grand certainties are dead. God. History. Truth. All dead. The weather—the seasons as we know them. Apparently even capitalism itself is dying!

Laughter.

Please! You wish!

Applause.

Oh, yes, it's an apocalypse, people! Well, you don't hear them complaining about the end of days in the wheat fields of Greenland. The Chinese and Mexicans are cloud seeding. Saudi Arabia is pioneering drought-resistant crop technology. They're growing food in dust bowls! If this is the apocalypse, I say bring it on!

It's time to embrace change and make practical preparations for our future.

Those of us gathered in this room are the solvers of the world's problems.

We are the pioneers.

The ones whose business acumen and innovation will help humanity adapt to the change that Mother Nature is wreaking upon us, even as we speak.

Loud cheers.

The timing is urgent.

VIKA *appears on the stage behind her. She walks slowly towards her, in the shadows.*

There are actually those—the enemy within—who would have us live in permanent terror and apprehension about the sort of change we are proposing this evening. Purveyors of doom who threaten us with violence for finding solutions to the world's problems!

Laughter and applause. VIKA *approaches her.*

Well, we're not afraid of you!

Cheers.

To this homegrown enemy, to the faceless and so-called 'cultural' terrorists, this 'Front', these Turquoise militants, I say … up yours! We are the history-makers. We are the gatekeepers. We are the future and we are unstoppable!

VIKA *presses a device cloaked within her clothes, around her chest. A massive bomb blast rips through the building. Screams. Sirens. Blackout.*

SCENE SIX

When the dust settles, we find BASRA *and* OLYMPIA *sitting in the lounge room with* JEFF. OLYMPIA *seems to be in some kind of trance. She has fallen asleep with her eyes open.*

BASRA: She was here. The whole time.
          Living with us.
          Planning it.
JEFF: Kinda spectacular when you think about it. The audacity of it.
BASRA: Infiltrated.
          Just like Grandma said they would.

Beat.

JEFF: Come here.

He gives her a bear hug.

You hangin' in there?

She nods.

You're safe.
BASRA: Am I?
JEFF: With me.

He goes to hug her again, but is unnerved by OLYMPIA *'s trance.*

Uh—is she okay?

BASRA: She falls asleep.

JEFF: Right.

BASRA: When she has the cochlear off too long. She forgets that she's awake.

JEFF: Okay.

> *Beat.*

What's the latest on your grandma?

BASRA: It's touch and go. They think they might be able to source most of the organs from the one person. She's on the top of the list.

JEFF: I bet she is! That machine your grandmother's on. I'll lay money on it having a Cleveland microchip inside it. So I guess you could say I'm helping.

> Yep. She may pull through after all.
>
> Isn't that great?
>
> [*To* OLYMPIA] Olympia?

He waves his hands in front of her eyes.

She never did this on the ship in the Arctic.

> She is alive, isn't she?

BASRA: I think so.

JEFF: How old is she exactly?

BASRA: [*with a shrug*] Ninety. A hundred. Immortal.

JEFF: Huh. Isn't that great?

> *Beat.*

Now, I know the timing of this statement might sound callous to you, Basra. But if your grandma dies, and once Miss Olympia here drops off her perch—God forbid—you stand to inherit your family's considerable wealth. You're going to be in a position to make all sorts of things possible …

BASRA: —

JEFF: Flipping the one per cent, remember?

BASRA: I—

OLYMPIA: Boom!

> *Beat. And back to her trance.*

JEFF: Is she …?

BASRA: She's fine. Look. Jeff. Now isn't the right—

JEFF: Now is the perfect time to strike.

BASRA: For me.

JEFF: To take advantage of the chaos on the streets.

BASRA: It isn't the right time for me.

JEFF: But if your grandmother dies, you'll have to take on the lobbying.

BASRA: For what?

JEFF: For New Eden. And help me identify pilgrims. The right kind. It seems to me that this here Front you talked about—the ones responsible for your grandma's accident—

BASRA: It was Visi who blew herself up. No group's claimed responsibility yet.

JEFF: Basra—maids don't have access to ballistics and explosives as a general rule.

　　Beat.

They may be the people we're looking for.

BASRA: I really don't think that's appropriate—

JEFF: You were a fan …

BASRA: Until I was their target.

JEFF: Your Grandma was the target.

BASRA: I feel betrayed.

JEFF: Sure. But … [*A different tack.*] You don't want to help anymore.

BASRA: No—that's not what I said.

JEFF: You've given up.

BASRA: I'm confused. Everything's upside down.

JEFF: Well now—one setback and you've given up. The paradigm programming kicks right back in, and the self-protection instinct takes over. I understand.

BASRA: —

OLYMPIA: [*suddenly*] The maid! She's back!

BASRA: Visi's dead, Aunt Olympia.

OLYMPIA: She's back.

JEFF: Not in one piece.

OLYMPIA: There on the street. In the lobby.

BASRA: You were just having a bad dream.

OLYMPIA: There was an elephant. A turquoise elephant roaming the streets of the city.

BASRA: They're hallucinations—

OLYMPIA: Everything upside down.

JEFF: The world's gone crazy, that's for sure. Hellfire and ruination!

The turquoise elephant appears.

OLYMPIA: No! No! Get it away from me!

BASRA: Olympia?

OLYMPIA: It's coming for me! The elephant. Get it away. Get it away!

BASRA: Aunt Olympia, wake up!

The elephant fades, and she's back in her trance again. JEFF *waves his hands across her eyes.*

JEFF: Well now. If that ain't the darndest thing.

BASRA: I should get her to bed.

JEFF: Sure. But this conversation isn't over, Basra. I'll talk you round. I know your life is in a state of flux, but you have a contribution to make. A vital one. I truly believe that. Lives don't just intersect like ours have for no reason. Your aunt and I being on that cruise. Meeting you all. Fate decreed it …

OLYMPIA *snaps out of her reverie.*

OLYMPIA: The elephant. It's delivered her.

BASRA: You were dreaming.

OLYMPIA: Here she is.

And in walks VISI.

Silence.

BASRA: It's not possible.

JEFF: Well, that is remarkable. Did you conjure her? I haven't seen that done outside of the Caribbean.

VISI: Please. I only have a few minutes. The security …

BASRA: How did you get through them? Are they all asleep? [*To* OLYMPIA] Call them!

OLYMPIA: They can't arrest a ghost!

VISI: I'm not a ghost.

BASRA: But you're dead.

OLYMPIA: [*to* JEFF] Her head landed in the fourteenth row.

VISI: It was Vika.

OLYMPIA: I was there. Saw it sail right past.

VISI: My sister.

BASRA: What?

VISI: My twin sister. Vika.

A pause as this sinks in.

She asked me all about you. Details about your grandmother's movements. Her schedule. We swapped places. On the way to the hotel.

BASRA: She was here?

VISI: Sometimes. Doing your grandmother's hair … Posting your video …

BASRA: That was her?

VISI: She said she was looking for the right opportunity. The right— what did she call it? The right forum.

BASRA: Then you're an accessory.

OLYMPIA: After the fact!

VISI: I didn't want her to do it.

OLYMPIA: Or possibly even before it. But what was the fact?

VISI: I didn't think it would happen.

OLYMPIA: The fact was her head landed in the fourteenth row.

JEFF: There's no getting around that.

VISI: Help me.

BASRA: We need to call them.

OLYMPIA: Who?

VISI: Please.

BASRA: Give me the phone.

OLYMPIA: Where is the phone?

BASRA: I'll buzz security.

OLYMPIA: What does it look like?

JEFF: Now hold on. Let's just hold on a minute. Basra—it seems to me that our friend here wants to make a deal.

BASRA: Short of selling us her internal organs, I'm not sure what it is she can do.

VISI: I can put you in touch with them.

Pause.

JEFF: Did you hear that, Basra? Visi has contacts.

VISI: I do. I can help you.

BASRA: Help me what?

VISI: Whatever you need.

JEFF: Contacts, Basra. Think of the contacts.

BASRA: I don't need The Front.

JEFF: I do. These Front people. They're the real deal. They're the sort of people who will give up everything to build a new community. This is the gene pool we need to start rebuilding from!

VISI: He's right.

BASRA: What are you talking about—gene pool? I thought we were taking in refugees. I thought New Eden was housing the displaced!

JEFF: They're warriors!

BASRA: They're murderers.

OLYMPIA: I'm confused. Whose side are we on?

BASRA: This woman plotted to kill your sister.

OLYMPIA: Well, that didn't work, did it?

VISI: She's alive?

OLYMPIA: Just.

BASRA: So it's only *attempted* murder you're an accomplice to now. Sleep well.

VISI: Then my sister died for nothing.

> *Beat.*

BASRA: Why are you here?

VISI: You're the only one who can help me.

BASRA: How do I know you're not still working for them?

VISI: I was never with The Front.

BASRA: How did you even get in here? The security codes. My God, she has our security codes! They all do!

JEFF: Oh, those can be changed.

VISI: Basra—please. I'm desperate.

BASRA: You really think I'll help you after—

VISI: Please. I thought we were friends. I thought we were—

BASRA: What?

OLYMPIA: Oh, this is all so tedious. I liked her better when she didn't speak.

JEFF: I think she's an innocent in all this. I really do.

BASRA: Yes, thanks, Jeff.

OLYMPIA: Was that her or the other one?

JEFF: I think she can help, Basra.

OLYMPIA: The one that didn't speak.

JEFF: I sniff win-win in all this.

BASRA: I don't. She was an accomplice to the planned *murder* of my grandmother.

OLYMPIA: To an acting Head of State.

BASRA: She can fuck off.

Beat.

VISI: Right. Okay. I guess that's the end of that, then.

BASRA: You think you can just leave?

VISI: Are you going to stop me?

Pause.

You've made a decision. Your political beliefs only seem to apply to other people's families. You'll house strangers in a fucking shack in the mountains, but you won't help me. So I'll leave and you can wrap yourself up in your fortress house and your wealth, and keep writing about turquoise elephants. It's words with all of you. 'Tisane' this and 'rococo' that …

BASRA: Don't you dare—my mother was a writer. My mother was a fucking Iraqi woman journalist who was killed—

VISI: You're a do-nothing—

BASRA: —not even you and your terrorist frauds could imagine—

VISI: A do-nothing, armchair—

BASRA: Excuse me, I'm talking. *I'm* talking.

Beat.

My mother had her throat sliced and her body pumped of blood— some *monster* stood on her stomach and pumped the blood from her body because she dared to criticise his cult in her newspaper. She was sacrificed on the fucking altar, Visi, in a way that makes your lot look like dilettantes. So don't you *dare* talk to me about wrapping myself up in a fortress. You are wrong about me. Wrong.

VISI: Prove it.

TRANSITION SEQUENCE:

Video sequence. The masked member of The Front again.

MASKED FIGURE: Rise up! *Rise up*, people!
>We're coming.
>For every one of you.
>Living in your ivory towers.
>Encased in your humidicribs and humidispheres.
>We'll hunt you down.
>One by one.
>When you're sleeping.
>In your beds.
>Behind your triple glazing.
>You won't know where to look.
>We'll be the ones throwing the bricks.
>We'll be the ones holding your hand in hospital.
>Adjusting your drips.
>Donating your organs.
>We'll be inside you next.
>You won't know where to fucking look.
>We're inside you.
>Do you get that?
>Inside you.

SCENE SEVEN

The doors blow open and AUGUSTA *hurtles into the room, bandaged head to toe. A pair of large, dark sunglasses are all that we see of her face. The same bouffant sticks out of the top of the bandages. A dramatic pause as the tumult dies down. And then, finally, she speaks:*

AUGUSTA: *Ich bin mit dem Schiff hierhergekommen. Die Jahreszeiten sind hier verkehrt herum. Nur die Kiefer sind mir bekannt.* [I arrived here on a boat. The seasons are upside down. Only the pine trees are familiar.]

>*A split second, and then* JEFF *enters, fiddling with a handheld device.*

JEFF: According to this machine, I think you just said you arrived here by a boat. The seasons are upside down. And only the pine trees are familiar.

AUGUSTA: Who are you?

JEFF: I'm the morning shift.

AUGUSTA: It feels like there's another person living inside my body.

JEFF: Apparently there are three. Donors, that is. Vying for internal supremacy.

AUGUSTA: Help me to the window.

He does.

I've never really looked at the city from here.

JEFF: Heatwaves and humanity as far as the eye can see. Not in New Eden though.

AUGUSTA: What's that?

JEFF: New Eden? Well, it's paradise. It will be. A fifty thousand square kilometre garden. Self-sustaining. Every tropical fruit and vegetable known to humanity. All that rain falling where it's never fallen before. We've got to get in. Before everyone else does.

AUGUSTA: Sounds urgent.

He pulls documents from his attaché case.

JEFF: Oh, yes, ma'am. And with your family's investment, and your government's permission, we'd own it. Secure. We'd build a dome.

AUGUSTA: My government?

JEFF: Yes, ma'am.

AUGUSTA: Am I still in government?

JEFF: [*offering her a pen*] Why, you're the interim Head of State, ma'am. They haven't had time to replace you. We were talking about this yesterday.

AUGUSTA: I don't know who you are.

JEFF: Sure you do. Remember? We're building a humidisphere. You're going to be safe there. It's a secret location.

AUGUSTA: Is it a retirement village?

JEFF: No! We hope most people there will be young. Breeding the next generation of ark-dwellers. Hell, we may even be starting a new species of man. And woman. A species content to get quiet, live simply—

without violence and hierarchy. A species devoted to peaceful thought and constructive rumination.

AUGUSTA: Like Trappist monks.

JEFF: Yeah, maybe. Maybe the species has already been invented.

AUGUSTA: And become extinct. Maybe you're just bringing it back from the brink.

JEFF: The other day—before your terrible accident—you asked me to book you a place on the ark.

AUGUSTA: I did?

JEFF: Yes, you were about to sign … [*showing the place on the document*] right here.

AUGUSTA: What was I signing?

JEFF: The document to the Minister recommending the release of the Crown land to me. He's been paralysed for weeks. Doesn't know what to do. But a recommendation from you would be all he needs to agree. Right here …

AUGUSTA: Are you sure?

JEFF: Basra believes in New Eden. Olympia believes in New Eden. We're all moving there together.

AUGUSTA: Well, if Basra agrees …

> *She signs the paper.* JEFF *turns each sheet of the document over for her to sign during the following.*

What will I do there?

JEFF: We'd find a good use for you.

AUGUSTA: I have … vague memories of being a pioneer. Arriving on a boat. In another city. With pine trees on the beach. It's all … just beyond the frontier of consciousness. It comes to me in the silent hours. Twilight. And dawn.

JEFF: There now. Getting quiet. That's the key to unlocking the Paradigm programming.

AUGUSTA: [*still signing*] I think we planted grapes. *Die Erde besteht aus Kalkstein und wird gut zu Weinbau passen.* [The soil is made of limestone. It will be good for wine.]

JEFF: Oops. I didn't get to this here translator in time. Was that something about wine?

AUGUSTA: [*suddenly distressed*] Where's Basra? And Olympia?

JEFF: Oh, don't you worry about that now. They're not far away. We're looking after you in shifts.

He gets the final copy signed and begins to slip the papers away out of sight in his case.

AUGUSTA: Do I know you? Are you the physiotherapist?

JEFF: Well—sure. If that makes you happy. I'm the physiotherapist.

AUGUSTA *relaxes, then spies something through the window.*

AUGUSTA: What's that?

JEFF: What's what?

AUGUSTA: On the street. There's an—an elephant. Do you see it?

JEFF: Where?

AUGUSTA: There. By the pavilion. An elephant.

JEFF: I don't—

AUGUSTA: It's blue.

JEFF: The pavilion?

AUGUSTA: The elephant. An aqua-coloured …

JEFF: Well now, that don't—

AUGUSTA: … turquoise-coloured … You must see it.

JEFF: [*genuinely trying*] I can't—

AUGUSTA: It's stopping traffic!

JEFF: Where?

AUGUSTA: There!

He can't see it.

Gone.

Silence.

There's a treaty.

JEFF: Say what now?

AUGUSTA: There's a treaty to be signed. It's urgent.

She is becoming distressed again. Wheeling around the room.

Everything's a jumble. It's all these … organs. I don't know who I am.

BASRA: [*entering*] That will be all, Jeff.

AUGUSTA: Oh, Basra. You'll know. I'm getting these memories of us being planters. Planters and harvesters.

BASRA: Who—the Macquaries?

AUGUSTA: But weren't we diggers?

BASRA: You name it, we've dug it up, stripped it bare and dispossessed whoever had it first.

AUGUSTA: Then who grew the wine?

BASRA: No idea.

AUGUSTA: It's important. And what's this treaty about?

BASRA: Don't get me started on the treaty.

AUGUSTA: I was supposed take something to Parliament. To persuade someone of something. Is there something else for me to sign, Jeff?

JEFF: …

BASRA: You need to relax, Grandma.

AUGUSTA: Why do you all change the subject when I mention the treaty?

JEFF: Because none of us agree with the damned thing.

AUGUSTA: I want to argue in favour of something none of you agree with?

BASRA: Pretty much.

AUGUSTA: And by 'none of us', who do you mean?

BASRA: No-one in this household. No-one with a right mind. No-one outside of big business and the fossil fuel industry.

AUGUSTA: Even Olympia?

BASRA: Oh, she doesn't care.

AUGUSTA: What's it about? Fossil fuels?

JEFF: A return to reliance on a finite, polluting resource. But really, none of it matters. The Earth is dying, the paradigm is collapsing and life as we know it is gonna end no matter what man does now. It's too late. No treaty one way or the other is gonna save or prolong a god-damn thing.

BASRA: That's nihilistic.

JEFF: It's the truth.

BASRA: I don't believe there's no hope.

JEFF: Paradigm self-talk. Good luck with that.

AUGUSTA: I don't understand. Are we all going to die? Is there something you're not telling me? A nuclear bomb? Terrorists …

BASRA: Grandma, why don't you go back to bed?

AUGUSTA: I can't sleep. The dreams …

BASRA: Or read.

AUGUSTA: Yes. I might do that. The orderly here just sold me a plot in his retirement village.

BASRA: He what?

JEFF: Our little joke.

AUGUSTA: He's building some kind of dome in the desert.

JEFF: I was telling her about New Eden.

BASRA: I'll bet.

AUGUSTA: He has my permission.

JEFF: A joke.

AUGUSTA: He says I'll be safe. From terrorists. Am I going to a commune?

BASRA: No, Grandma.

AUGUSTA: Why not?

BASRA: Because you *hate*—

AUGUSTA: What? Hate what?

> *Pause.*

Tell me. Please. I can't remember.

BASRA: Never mind. You need to rest now.

AUGUSTA: Good.

> *Beat.*

Ja, gut.

> *Beat.*

BASRA: How much longer will you be here, Jeff?

JEFF: As soon as I've bought the land, we'll leave.

BASRA: 'We'?

JEFF: Well, you're coming, aren't you?

BASRA: That was before—

JEFF: And Miss Olympia. I'll take Visi too.

AUGUSTA: The maid?

BASRA: Yes.

AUGUSTA: The sister of the terrorist?

BASRA: The accomplice, yes.

AUGUSTA: You know where she is? In prison?

> BASRA *exchanges a glance with* JEFF.

BASRA: You could say she's under house arrest.

AUGUSTA: But I'm alive. Did she commit a crime or not?

BASRA: It's not black and white.

AUGUSTA: She's either innocent or she isn't.

> *Pause.*

BASRA: She might be.

JEFF: I think she is.

AUGUSTA: Did I like her?

BASRA: I think so.

AUGUSTA: So, she's probably innocent, we all liked her, and she's in jail for killing someone who's still alive?

> *Beat.*

BASRA: She's not in prison.

AUGUSTA: You just said she was under house arrest.

> BASRA *nods to* JEFF. *He exits.*

BASRA: I wasn't sure whether to tell you or not.

AUGUSTA: Tell me what?

BASRA: Whether it would upset you …

AUGUSTA: Basra dear, you're really going to have to stop talking in riddles. I'm not a child. I've just survived a close-range bombing. I think I can withstand whatever truth it is you're concealing from me—

> VISI *enters the room, followed silently by* JEFF.

Well now.
  Well now.

VISI: Hello.

AUGUSTA: Hello.

BASRA: Half the country's looking for her.

JEFF: No hope of finding her though in this chaos. She's escaped. To the wilds.

AUGUSTA: Has she?

BASRA: So what do you think?

AUGUSTA: Are you a hardened criminal?

> VISI *shrugs.*

I think I was hardened too.
  From all accounts.

I had a son.
Someone killed him.
A suicide bomber.
BASRA: That was twenty years ago, Grandma.
AUGUSTA: And then I became hard.
BASRA: You don't like talking about it.
AUGUSTA: Talking about what?
BASRA: Daddy. The past.
AUGUSTA: All this hardening.
It has to stop.
And now I'd like to be alone, please.
Alone to watch the view.

JEFF, VISI *and* BASRA *exit.*

AUGUSTA *watches the sunset—an intense flood of reds and oranges bathe her. She stares at it in wonder.*

I had a son.
Oh, Duncan.
What have I become?
I've been wrong. About everything.

TRANSITION SEQUENCE:

MASKED FIGURE: The mayhem continues, people! We blow up one fascist, and another one takes their place. The whole system is infested with vested interests and they keep proliferating.

They're signing over the deserts to developers. Quashing native title. Dispossessing the First Nations all over again. Signing the land over to foreign snake-oil investors. Some American whack job building a giant glass dome over half of the Northern Territory!

It's just you and us and the whackos now, fighting over what's left.
This is a battle for survival, people.
A battle over resources.
A battle over the scraps.
Rise up and take back what's yours!
Rise up and—

Cut.

SCENE EIGHT

JEFF, VISI, OLYMPIA *and* BASRA *are in the room together.* JEFF *is holding court.* AUGUSTA *is separate to the main group, gazing out the window.*

JEFF: Here are the drawings! There will be towers that draw in humidity from the atmosphere and channel it back inside the dome through subterranean vectors. Channel it back as fresh water. The whole system is self-sustaining. We got the technology from Singapore. Oh, it's so close now I can almost taste it!

And—you'll like this, Visi—we've made arrangements with the First Nations people in the area. The ones whose land has been donated. We'll provide sanctuary to any of them who donate their labour to aid in the construction.

VISI: You won't pay them?

JEFF: We're providing something more valuable than cash.

VISI: You've taken their land—

JEFF: Been given.

VISI: Taken their land and now you're exploiting their labour? What was there in that arrangement that you thought I'd like?

JEFF: It's bartering. An exchange economy. We're stepping outside of the capitalist paradigm.

OLYMPIA: Is the amber concubine going to be there?

JEFF: There'll be hundreds of amber concubines, Olympia.

BASRA: What do you mean—hundreds of concubines?

JEFF: It's a new world we're building.

BASRA: And is that what I am? And Visi too?

JEFF: Of course not. Well—not *just* that.

OLYMPIA: Where do I fit in?

JEFF: Wherever you like.

OLYMPIA: I don't like the sound of that. This New Eden is beginning to sound degenerate.

JEFF: O brave new world—

BASRA/VISI: —that has such people in it.

Beat. They stare at each other. An accidental synergy.

JEFF: A brave new world. I'll be Prospero and Visi here will be Miranda.

OLYMPIA: I thought I was Miranda.

JEFF: Oh, you're my favourite wood nymph! You're my Ariel!

OLYMPIA: The one who was stuck in a tree?

JEFF: We're going to Eden, folks! It's really happening!

OLYMPIA: Ariel. I don't even think it was female.

JEFF: What do you think, Augusta? Will you come too?

Pause.

AUGUSTA: Yes.

BASRA: What?! Grandma, don't be ridiculous.

AUGUSTA: I want to become a pioneer again. Like my ancestors.

JEFF: Happy day!

BASRA: Those are your organs speaking. They're not your memories.

AUGUSTA: Nonsense. You can't inherit memory.

BASRA: You're not well.

AUGUSTA: I'm going to Eden.

BASRA: But you'd never—

AUGUSTA: The old Augusta would never. But the old Augusta is gone, Basra. She was blown up and good riddance to her. Build me a luxury suite, Jeff. With a view.

JEFF: I'll build you anything you want! I'll name half the colony after you!

OLYMPIA: Port Augusta!

JEFF: Mount Olympia!

OLYMPIA: Miranda! Miranda!

OLYMPIA/AUGUSTA: Where are you, Miranda?!

BASRA *and* VISI *look on warily at the elders' tea party. A dizzy dance.*

A buzzer goes off, like before.

OLYMPIA: Ring the alarum! Oh! It's New Guinea. There's a glacier melting.

JEFF: They have glaciers in New Guinea?

OLYMPIA: Not for much longer.

AUGUSTA: You can't leave now, Olympia.

OLYMPIA: You're right. I'm sick of glaciers melting. Besides—I just bought a kakapo. From New Zealand. I thought you might roast it, Visi.

BASRA: She's not the cook anymore.

OLYMPIA: Stuff it with macadamias.

JEFF: Bring it to New Eden!

AUGUSTA: Bring two—a breeding pair!

OLYMPIA: We'll eat all the endangered species back into existence.

JEFF: Dodos!

AUGUSTA: And thylacines!

JEFF: White tigers!

OLYMPIA: White rhinos!

AUGUSTA: And turquoise elephants!

OLYMPIA: All aboard!

AUGUSTA: All aboard!

JEFF/OLYMPIA/AUGUSTA: All aboard!

A dance macabre.

VISI: Stop!

Silence.

You're all crazy!

A pause as everyone stops and stares at her.

Why are you doing this?

AUGUSTA: To set things straight.

VISI: What things? None of this makes sense. You: [OLYMPIA] Stop eating kakapo. Buy a fucking chicken. Eat Red Rooster. They cook it for you. Stop deluding yourself you're a concubine. He just wants your money. He thinks you'll be dead before you get there. You: [JEFF] Get on your jeep and go to your giant dome and jack yourself off in the wilderness. Stop pretending you're God. You're a fucking crackpot. You: [AUGUSTA] Stop pretending you see elephants on the street. There's nothing there. You're as crazy as he is. I liked you better when you were a right-wing bitch. At least then you were consistent. And you: [BASRA] Snap the fuck out of it. This man's not saving humanity. He's just keeping the bits of it he likes. 'New Eden'? Yeah, right. The old one worked out so well! It's a white man's cock fantasy, Basra! Concubines and slaves. Are you fucking kidding me? I don't know what the solutions to your problems are, but I can tell you one thing: this dick and his dome in the desert are not it.

Stunned silence. BASRA *knows* VISI *is right.*

JEFF: Well now. Thank you for sharing your opinions with us, Visi. We appreciate your honesty.

OLYMPIA: Do you really want me to drop dead, Jeff?

JEFF: Of course not.

OLYMPIA: I don't know if I can come along if that's the case. I might have to go to New Guinea instead.

VISI: Are you listening to this, Basra? They're all deluded.

AUGUSTA: The elephants aren't delusions, Visi. They're real. I've seen them with my own eyes.

OLYMPIA: I've seen them too.

VISI: Basra?

OLYMPIA: What do they mean?

JEFF: That the paradigm is coming to a close. It's ending. The ark is about to set sail!

VISI: You can't sail an ark into the fucking desert, Jeff!

AUGUSTA: I need to speak to Parliament. I need to set things right.

BASRA: Grandma, you can't.

AUGUSTA: I can. And I will. I've made up my mind. I need to tell the world about the elephants.

VISI: [*to* BASRA] This is a lunatic asylum. You need to get out.

SCENE NINE

AUGUSTA *is stripped bare of bandages. She is in parliament. The sounds of ayes and nays and hear-hears rise and subside. She approaches a podium, a walking stick propping her up.*

AUGUSTA: Members of Parliament, Prime Minister. I thank you for allowing me to petition you on behalf of the delegates that I represent. I nearly didn't make it. A bit of trouble with the hired help.

Cheers and laughter.

Every nation on every continent has been dramatically affected by what we've called Climate Change. That is not under dispute. Some nations have learned to adapt to changing conditions. Indeed, some have flourished. Others have perished and ceased to exist. It is a chaotic and alarming time. A time for urgency and quick thinking.

And a time for far-reaching vision because Lord knows it is a time of far-reaching consequences.

Hear-hear!

You all know what I stand for. You know what I am going to say.

Pause.

Or so you think.

I have had a change of heart.

Quite literally.

Someone else's heart. Someone else's liver and lungs, someone else's kidneys—someone else has donated a life in order for an old woman to survive on a planet that she will surely not live to see survive beyond another decade or two.

But you all have to live with it for the rest of your lives. As do your descendants.

Mixed murmurings of assent and dissent—consternation perhaps.

I have had a change of heart and a change of mind.

For I have seen the turquoise elephant roaming our streets.

The hubbub and murmurings have died down now and there is absolute silence.

The elephant has arrived in the room.

It's here.

It's here.

Can you see it?

Beautiful.

Those eyes. Mournful. Pleading. Expressive. 'Help me,' its eyes say, 'I am the first and last of my kind. I am unique.'

Becoming disoriented. The elephant retreats.

Don't go!

There was a constant syllabub that rose above the bowl's meniscus. A rosewater syllabub more constant than any Eton's mess. An Eton's mess, an evening dress, a hubbub and a fizzwhiz. A whirligig.

The cabriolet was lagan on the klep is shmorg to flapencroft. Kapakapa weewak. A fizzibub ... a fizzy fizz ... a fizzer ... fizza fizza ...

She collapses. Sirens. Darkness.

TRANSITION SEQUENCE:

MASKED FIGURE: [*deranged now, unhinged*] Hate to crash the party, people. Sorry to cut the doomsday prognostications short.

But look at the weather charts.

There are superstorm cells building along the entire of the east coast. Moving down, port by port.

Swimming pools tumbling off cliffs and into the surf.

Things are about to get dark.

Very dark.

Take advantage of the mayhem!

Now is the time to strike!

Before Parliament gets a chance to vote.

Every power station in the country.

Every symbol of power and decadence.

All at once.

Every member of The Front.

Donating.

Everything.

At once.

Here's a little taste of what's to come.

We see the Sydney Harbour Bridge.

Sssshhh.

Pay attention.

Hold your breath.

Suddenly the bridge explodes in an orange fireball.

We call this installation 'Bridge Over Troubled Waters'.

Sayonara, sleepers.

Over and out.

SCENE TEN

BASRA, JEFF *and* OLYMPIA *are in the living room.*

JEFF: I've bought a jeep and enough gas to get us to Timbuktu. We'll be New Eden's first pilgrims.

BASRA: What—and sleep alone together under the stars while the dome magically materialises around us? While your black slaves fan us and feed us by hand?

JEFF: The pilgrims are descending. We have a green light on this. I'm offering you a ticket out of here.

BASRA: I don't think so, Jeff.

JEFF: You've got less than ten minutes to decide, Basra. Choose life over death. Come with us and start a new world. This one is about to fall apart. It's the end.

BASRA: I don't believe that.

JEFF: It's the end of everything you know to be real and safe.

BASRA: I can't just run away and hide.

JEFF: What's the alternative?

BASRA: To fight. To overturn the bill. To—

JEFF: What? To build solar panels. Recycle? Plant a few more trees? Blog about it?

OLYMPIA: I might go to New Guinea after all.

BASRA: It's better than running.

OLYMPIA: You wouldn't miss me, would you?

JEFF: The machine is shutting down.

> *Beat.*

There's nothing here for you.

Who are you staying for?

The ghost who walks here will be dead any tick of the clock.

BASRA: Jeff!

JEFF: Oh, she can't hear me. And your grandmother has just been exposed on global television as a gabbling crackpot. 'Fizzy whizz! Fizz bang!' What the fuck? Come on! She'll never work again. She's done. She'll be asked to step down by the end of the week.

> BASRA *does not respond.*

Look, I won't lie to you. You can stay here and die along with everyone else. But there's a hell of a lot you can do for humanity at New Eden with ten billion bucks. Come with me, Basra. Come and be part of the one per cent.

BASRA/OLYMPIA: Visi was right.

BASRA: You're a fraud.

OLYMPIA: The ghost who walks is switching you off.

OLYMPIA flicks a switch on her cochlear and retreats to her inner world.

The door blasts open—the gales we saw billowing earlier announce the entrance of a refreshed-looking AUGUSTA.

AUGUSTA: It was an air bubble!

Beat.

In my brain. It was air bubbles all along.

BASRA: What are you talking about?

AUGUSTA: Air bubbles in the bloodstream. After a major operation. Perfectly normal. They short-circuit the neural transmitters. I was seeing things that weren't there. And then when I was giving the speech to Parliament. Perhaps it was the strain of the occasion. My blood pressure higher than normal. But one of them popped. Inside my brain. That's what caused the spiels of drivel. The hallucination. And now it's out. The oxygen. Exhumed. Expunged! I'm back to normal. Everything back to normal. Isn't that just marvellous?

Beat.

Something smells.

OLYMPIA: That's last night's dinner.

AUGUSTA: Like old prawns.

OLYMPIA: Yes. We had Patagonian toothfish.

Follows her nose.

AUGUSTA: Not that. It's not coming from the kitchen. It's …

She's arrived at JEFF.

Oh. Who are you?

JEFF: Why, I'm Jeff Cleveland. You don't remember me?

AUGUSTA: You smell dreadful. Hasn't anyone shown you the shower?

JEFF: I told you. I choose not to bathe in artificial or treated water, Mrs Macquarie.

AUGUSTA: 'Your Excellency'.

JEFF: Ma'am.

AUGUSTA: Then you can stand outside until it rains. Visi! Where is she?

BASRA: She spends all her time in your bunker. On the computer.

AUGUSTA: Plotting.

BASRA: Bored. Trapped. Like the rest of us.

AUGUSTA: Speak for yourself. Visi!

> VISI *enters.*

Ah, here she is. Visi, it's been lovely, dear, but we won't be requiring your services any longer. Housing the relative of a terrorist who attempted to blow me to smithereens makes absolutely no sense. I'll contact security and let them know you're here.

BASRA: Excuse me?

AUGUSTA: [*to* VISI] I'll have Gregor drive you to the nearest police station once he's dropped me off at the airport. It would be better if you turned yourself in. Kept us out of things.

BASRA: No!

VISI: I told you.

BASRA: That isn't fair!

AUGUSTA: It's not just fair, it's legally correct, Basra. Stop wailing like a Mediterranean and face up to your responsibilities.

JEFF: This is all cockeyed logic.

AUGUSTA: Why are you still here?

JEFF: Well now. I thought we'd developed a friendship. A spiritual connection forged over humidispheres and luxury suites.

AUGUSTA: You developed a bond with an air bubble, Mr Cleveland. Not with me.

JEFF: That disappoints me to hear you say it. You told me about your memories of a legacy that were coming back to you. Norfolk pine trees … Arriving ashore in a boat …

AUGUSTA: Those were hallucinations.

JEFF: … on a beach with a name that was spelt the same forwards and backwards. A free state without the taint of convict history …

AUGUSTA: I really don't …

BASRA: You spoke German.

AUGUSTA: I told you that was the air bubble.

OLYMPIA: We've never learned German.

AUGUSTA: Everyone picks up a few words here and there.

JEFF: Common, found phrases …

AUGUSTA: Yes.

JEFF: Like 'The soil is made of limestone'.
AUGUSTA: Well—
OLYMPIA: That was clever.
JEFF: And 'The seasons are upside down'.
OLYMPIA: I wonder how she did it.
AUGUSTA: [*becoming agitated*] I told you, that was the drugs they had me on. The treatment.
JEFF: Drugs don't teach you languages you've never spoken.
AUGUSTA: The—the organs then.
JEFF: Language recollection is stored in the liver and pancreas?
AUGUSTA: Maybe.
JEFF: In the heart.
BASRA: Not the brain?
AUGUSTA: Well, it sounds preposterous when you put it like that.
OLYMPIA: I blame the doctors. In cahoots with the terrorists!
AUGUSTA: No, no. There was no German. No seasons. No elephants. No—

Silence.

A turquoise elephant enters the room—faintly, quietly—and stares at AUGUSTA. *She and* OLYMPIA *are the only ones who see it.*

You.
OLYMPIA: There!
JEFF: Mrs Macquarie?
OLYMPIA: It's here!
AUGUSTA: No! I won't have it.
BASRA: Grandma?
OLYMPIA: I need to censor it!
AUGUSTA: I won't see it.
OLYMPIA: Turn it off!
AUGUSTA: I refuse!
OLYMPIA: Turn it off!
AUGUSTA: Refuse, do you hear me? I deny you!
OLYMPIA: Shoo! Shoo!
AUGUSTA: I deny you!

She has seen the elephant off.

There!

JEFF: Why don't you go lie down awhile?

AUGUSTA: That's the way to deal with that!

OLYMPIA: Didn't anyone else see it?

JEFF: Visi here can show you to your room.

AUGUSTA: Visi's going to prison. And you're leaving too, you grotty little man. And by the way, I have revoked your purchase of the Crown land you wanted in Central Australia. Remember those documents you got me to sign when I was medically and mentally unfit? I told the minister I signed under duress. He's torn up your contract. Null. And. Void. So that puts an end to that fantasy.

JEFF: You can't. I've bought it. I own it.

AUGUSTA: You own what your fellow countrymen like to refer to as 'jack shit', Mr Cleveland. Oh—and you're about to be served a summons for outstaying your visa. You're an illegal immigrant. Get out while you can. Now! I'm returning to the capital and watching the vote from the gallery.

BASRA: You're still hallucinating. You need rest.

AUGUSTA: Nonsense. Rest is for the decrepit and the unemployed. That's all I came here to say. I've got a flight to Canberra that leaves in an hour. [*To* VISI] Deal with this mess while I'm gone, will you?

> AUGUSTA *is almost at the door.*

BASRA: You know you're lying. You and all your coal industry execs and CEOs. You all know deep in your hearts that the science is true.

AUGUSTA: Do we, Basra?

BASRA: Yes. I'd actually have more respect for you if you just came clean and admitted that your investment in all this is purely financial. If you just admitted that we're the ones who caused all this. But that you just don't give a shit.

AUGUSTA: Would that really make you happy, Basra?

BASRA: Yes.

AUGUSTA: Really?

BASRA: Yes.

> *Beat.*

AUGUSTA: Okay.
    We did this.
    We did it, Basra.

And I just don't give a shit.

They look each other in the eye. AUGUSTA *sweeps from the house.*

JEFF: The bitch shafted me!

VISI: You're a creep, Jeff. A creep with a Messiah complex and a jeep.

BASRA: So fuck off and never come back.

JEFF: Miss Olympia—

OLYMPIA: Oh, don't look at me, dear. I can't hear a word you're saying. Had my cochlear edit you out twenty minutes ago. You're just an empty mouth flapping on a stick.

JEFF: I see.

OLYMPIA: Flap flap.

JEFF: Well now …

I see.

Enjoy the view from the *Titanic*, ladies.

You're all going down.

VISI: Yeah—but not on you.

JEFF *leaves.*

BASRA: Why didn't you leave with him?

That was your 'get out of jail free' card.

VISI *shrugs.*

VISI: It's better like this.

BASRA: Why?

VISI: It's truthful.

OLYMPIA*'s buzzer goes off.*

OLYMPIA: Oh! Where to next?

BASRA: I don't know how to help you now. Not now that my grandmother's—herself again.

VISI: I knew she'd change back.

OLYMPIA: What? No, that can't be right.

VISI: You didn't buy it, did you? The mad hatter's fucking tea party. The family trip to Eden.

BASRA: I guess I hoped that—

VISI: What?

OLYMPIA: Sydney, Australia!

BASRA: There'd be a middle path. A sensible—

VISI: There hasn't been a middle path for decades.

OLYMPIA: It says that everyone's coming here.

Sound of an angry mob picks up from the streets again.

VISI: They're back.

   The people.

OLYMPIA: Oh, goody goody goody!

VISI: They're angry again.

OLYMPIA: Now this is going to be something.

VISI: Blocking that treaty was their last hope.

OLYMPIA: A superstorm! Thirteen-metre swells. Right here in the harbour!

VISI: They see your house, your glass palace, looking down over the harbour, and they want to smash bricks through it.

OLYMPIA: I'm going to have the best seat in the house.

   OLYMPIA *exits.*

VISI: They know who you are.

   You're still the enemy.

The mob get wilder. A brick hits the triple glazing.

What are you going to do?

With your millions and billions.

BASRA: I'll buy land. Buy forests. Preserve everything.

VISI: A week. A fortnight ago I would have believed you. But it's all changed. There's nothing left to spend it on. Nothing it can save. Not now.

BASRA: Well, not if it's as bad as you all say it is.

VISI: You don't even know, do you?

   What it's like out there?

   When was the last time you left this house?

Beat.

Oh, my God. You haven't—

   It's been months, hasn't it?

   Years?

BASRA: —

VISI: That's just fucking weird, Basra.

   It's sick.

Another brick against the glass.

This is the last time I'll see you.

BASRA: You can keep coming.

VISI: We both know that's not true.

I knew.

That this was the last time.

I got the driver—Gregor.

He's been helping me.

BASRA: What do you mean?

VISI: He's on our side.

He's joined us.

BASRA: Who's 'us'?

VISI: Who do you think?

BASRA: Oh, my God. Grandma—

Beat.

VISI: I'm sorry.

She opens her jacket. It is lined with explosives. She approaches
BASRA. BASRA *is rooted to the spot.*

Every member of The Front is doing this.

At power stations. Transmitters. Banks. Big businesses. Everything
that pollutes and corrupts us.

Tonight.

Right around the country.

*We think she is about to detonate the explosives. Instead she takes
the jacket off and hands it over to* BASRA.

This one's for you.

You said you were an activist.

Goodbye, Basra.

She exits silently.

She leaves the door open.

The turquoise elephant appears. BASRA *finally sees it.*

OLYMPIA *enters with a chair and lorgnette and fan. She pops herself by the window, fans herself and looks at the harbour through
her lorgnette.*

OLYMPIA: The Opera House is going under.

> Disappearing forever.
>
> During the storm.
>
> Isn't that exciting?
>
> Will you sit here with me and watch it, Basra dear?

BASRA: I'm don't know.

OLYMPIA: You're not going out?

> Oh, silly me. You never go out, do you?
>
> Not for years.
>
> Not since you were a little girl.
>
> You're a watcher.
>
> Like me.
>
> We're watchers, you and I.
>
> Oh! There! Look! You can see it coming up now!
>
> The water.
>
> It's on the concourse.
>
> Where's the Harbour Bridge gone?
>
> Are you going out, dear, or staying in?

BASRA: I—

BASRA stares from the elephant to the door—torn between the two.

OLYMPIA: Get a chair and sit next to me.

> This is going to be the best one yet!
>
> Better than Melbourne.
>
> Better than Kilimanjaro.
>
> This will even be better than the Sphinx.

As OLYMPIA *peers at the carnage through her lorgnette, the elephant sheds a tear and its image fills the room.*

Lights fade on BASRA *staring at the door.*

THE END

LADIES DAY
Alana Valentine

It's Ladies Day at the Broome races and the divinely beautiful Mike is the toast of the track. But amongst the froth and festivity, a brutal act of violence reminds us that life is not just all swishy hemlines, debonair gents and fascinators galore. Known for her successful verbatim works, Alana Valentine takes her interviews and research with individuals and communities, and mixes them with a healthy dose of drama.

978-1-92500-564-6, also available as a digital edition

REPLAY
Phillip Kavanagh

John saw his brother Michael die. He seems to have forgotten it, until now. His brother Peter saw it too, but remembers things differently. Together, they revisit the past in search of a common truth. But this search has terrifying, unexpected consequences for them both. Winner of the Patrick White Playwrights' Award in 2011.

978-1-92500-573-8, also available as a digital edition

THE LITERATI
Justin Fleming after Molière

Juliet and Clinton are in love. Guileless, sweet, all-encompassing love. However, love is not without its impediments. Standing in the way of their eternal happiness are Juliet's mother and sister, whose disapproval is of the most high-brow kind. Justin Fleming has audaciously brought Molière's *Les Femmes Savantes* (The Learned Ladies) screaming into the 21st century and created a sassy, Sydney story filled with linguistic dexterity, wit and rhyme.

978-1-92500-569-1, also available as a digital edition

GLORIA
Benedict Andrews

Playing the real-life survivor of a sadistic crime, Gloria must immerse herself in the horror of her character's reality. As she falls further into the abyss, the unravelling of her mind is reflected by the breakdown of order around her. We see a portrait of a society afraid to acknowledge its widening gaps. A beautifully complex and original work, *Gloria* is at once deeply Australian yet global in its perspective.

978-1-92500-568-4

www.ingramcontent.com/pod-product-compliance
Lightning Source LLC
Chambersburg PA
CBHW050022090426
42734CB00021B/3377

* 9 7 8 1 9 2 5 0 0 5 7 4 5 *